ARGENTINA

TITLES IN THE MODERN NATIONS OF THE WORLD SERIES INCLUDE:

Afghanistan	Kenya
Australia	Lebanon
Austria	Mexico
Brazil	Nigeria
Cambodia	Norway
Canada	Pakistan
China	Peru
Cuba	Philippines
Czech Republic	Poland
England	Russia
Ethiopia	Saudi Arabia
Finland	Scotland
France	Somalia
Germany	South Africa
Greece	South Korea
Haiti	Spain
Hungary	Sweden
India	Switzerland
Iran	Taiwan
Iraq	Thailand
Ireland	Turkey
Israel	United States
Italy	Vietnam
Japan	Yemen
Jordan	

ARGENTINA

BY TERRI DOUGHERTY

LUCENT BOOKS®

THOMSON

GALE

San Diego • Detroit • New York • San Francisco • Cleveland • New Haven, Conn. • Waterville, Maine • London • Munich

THOMSON

GALE

™

On Cover: A busy street in Buenos Aires glows at sunset.

LIBRARY OF CONGRESS CATALOGING-IN-PUBLICATION DATA

Dougherty, Terri.
  Argentina / by Terri Dougherty.
     p. cm. — (Modern nations of the world)
Summary: Examines the land, people, history, politics, culture, and
contemporary daily life of Argentina.
Includes bibliographical references and index.
  ISBN 1-59018-108-5 (hardback : alk. paper)
1. Argentina—Juvenile literature. [1. Argentina.] I. Title. II.
Series.
F2808.2.D68 2003
982—dc21
                                                                        2002156785

Printed in the United States of America

CONTENTS

INTRODUCTION   6
    Argentina: A World Apart

CHAPTER ONE   10
    A Diverse Landscape

CHAPTER TWO   23
    A Tumultuous Beginning

CHAPTER THREE   35
    Persistent Peronism

CHAPTER FOUR   51
    Daily Life in Argentina

CHAPTER FIVE   66
    Arts and Culture

CHAPTER SIX   80
    Contemporary Challenges

    Facts About Argentina   89
    Notes   92
    Chronology   94
    Glossary   99
    For Further Reading   101
    Works Consulted   102
    Index   105
    Picture Credits   111
    About the Author   112

INTRODUCTION

ARGENTINA: A WORLD APART

Argentina is a South American country that seems to form a world all of its own. Its landscape covers a range of climates and topography while its culture reflects the influences of both its Latin American and European roots. The vibrant coastal city of Buenos Aires is a cosmopolitan hub, while the smaller cities of the interior of the country contain a mixture of native and Hispanic influences, in addition to the cultures of other immigrant groups. Argentina is a land that has produced tango dancers, gauchos, and beef grilled to perfection. Its people expect great things of a nation that has an abundance of food and other natural resources; they are a proud population. Yet it is also a country that is often held back by political tension or economic problems, as if it cannot quite decide what to do with the wide variety of resources it has at its disposal.

At times, it seems as though Argentina wishes it were part of Europe. Buildings and boulevards in Buenos Aires, its capital city, are reminiscent of Paris. Its ice cream is like that of Italy. It has Welsh chapels and tea houses. Part of the reason for its European leanings is that Argentina's people are mainly of European descent, unlike in other countries in South America. It is said that Bolivians and Peruvians descended from the Inca, Guatemalans descended from the Maya, Mexicans descended from the Aztec, and Argentines descended from boats. The varied backgrounds of Argentina's people add another layer of complexity to a multifaceted country.

GREAT WEALTH AND POLITICAL INSTABILITY

Both the prospect of great wealth and recurring political instability have been hallmarks of Argentina's history. The country has many natural resources, and the potential for their use causes the people to hope that they will profit from the nation's environmental bounty. However, these hopes are almost inevitably dashed by the country's inability to properly use the resources for the good of the nation. Argentina's leaders have traditionally looked at what is best for themselves or a particular region of the nation, rather than the best way to use the natural resources for the good of the country as a whole. The people of the coastal city of Buenos Aires, the nation's capital and largest city, are proud of their status and believe that the wealth and power of the nation should be centered there. Those who live inland believe that they should be allowed to make their own decisions and not be strictly supervised by a strong central government. Failure to achieve a lasting balance between these two factions has been a persistent problem.

There have been political disagreements in this region of South America since the days of Spanish colonialism. In modern times, Argentina's military leaders have played an active role in politics, and in the name of protecting the people from internal revolt as well as outside threats, the army has not hesitated to oust established political regimes by force. Although there has been a respite from military coups during the past twenty years, the nation still faces destabilizing problems such as corruption within its government.

The architecture of Buenos Aires, the capital city of Argentina, reflects the European heritage of most Argentines.

Despite conflicts within its leadership, Argentina has managed at times to be a thriving nation. The century-old phrase "rich as an Argentine" reflects the respect the rest of the world once had for Argentina's citizens. In the late 1800s and early 1900s it was looked upon as one of the richest countries in the world. Its citizens have typically enjoyed a higher standard of living than those in other Latin American countries. Boasting nearly universal literacy, Argentina has long had an educated middle class which could afford the luxuries of developed nations. Yet economic problems have persisted throughout its history. Eager to please those who have the power to keep them in office and tempted to serve the interests of one group over those of another, its leaders have been unable to sustain prolonged economic success. The country has gone from a nation with one of the world's wealthiest economies to one where growing poverty is becoming a serious problem. Unemployment, misuse of public funds, persistent economic problems, and a growing feeling of despair are making it difficult for Argentines to return to the comfortable lifestyle they had in the past.

A young couple dances the tango, the expressive national dance of Argentina.

A NATION STILL APART

Argentina has prided itself on being set apart from other Latin American nations, and its distinct cultural contributions still shine. Its gauchos reflect a spirit of freedom. Its national dance, the tango, is a sultry outlet of self-expression. The citizens of Buenos Aires are proud to live in one of the most cosmopolitan cities in the world. Yet its status as a wealthy nation with a strong middle class is in jeopardy.

Argentina is a land of contrasts and contradictions. Its landscape is in some places beautiful, fertile, and developed, in other places barren and desolate. It is capable of producing an abundance of food, yet in some areas of the nation a number of children are starving. It has the opportunity to make use of natural resources, yet it must cope with severe economic and political problems. But although Argentina's people come from a variety of countries and cultures, they are emphatically Argentine. They want to tap into the potential their country holds, but until its leaders come to understand how to pull together the country's many resources and put them to their best use, Argentina's future remains uncertain. Allowing much of the country's potential to remain stagnant could spell disaster. If Argentina is to return to its former glory, its leaders will have to form a cohesive plan of action that benefits the many elements of the nation's culture.

1

A Diverse Landscape

Argentina is a wedge-shaped country in the southern half of South America. The eighth-largest country in the world, it stretches about 2,300 miles from north to south, longer than the continental United States. The country's 1.1 million square miles contain a varied landscape of fertile farmland, barren deserts, tropical jungles, soaring mountains, and swampy lowlands. Argentina's geography is diverse, rich, and beautiful, and supports a variety of plant and animal life. Glaciers and ice fields, deep blue glacial lakes, and windswept plains are part of a land that is both appealing and forbidding.

Second in size only to Brazil in South America, Argentina is bordered by Bolivia, Paraguay, Brazil, and Uruguay to the north and northeast. Chile is to the west, and the Atlantic Ocean washes against its eastern coast. The Andes Mountains stretch along its border with Chile.

As is true of all countries south of the equator, Argentina's seasons are the reverse of those in North America. Its hottest days are in January and February, while its coldest are in July and August. The climate is mainly temperate. Temperatures in northern Argentina average 77 degrees Fahrenheit in summer and drop to 55 degrees in winter. However, the average temperature drops as one goes south. In Patagonia, temperatures average 70 degrees in summer and 35 degrees in winter. On the foggy island of Tierra del Fuego, in the southernmost part of Argentina, summertime highs average only 52 degrees. The winter temperature on the island is moderated by the ocean, and dips to an average of 40 degrees.

Argentina's name comes from the Latin word for silver, *argentum*. The Spanish explorers who named the region were impressed by the silver ornaments worn by natives and believed they would be able to find much silver there. While they were wrong about the silver, the explorers had entered a diverse land rich in many other resources.

MESOPOTAMIA

Argentina's northeast is colored with the lush, tropical beauty of a rain forest. Vegetation, including ferns, orchids, and begonias, thrives in the damp climate. Much of the region is a subtropical jungle and is covered with lagoons and marshes. Bordered by the Paraná and Uruguay Rivers, it is called Mesopotamia from the Greek words for "middle" and "rivers." However, it should not be confused with the ancient Mesopotamia region in the Middle East. Argentina's Mesopotamia is a present-day, rural region with marshes, beaches, and jungle. There are no large urban areas in the region, mainly towns and small cities such as Paraná, with 210,000 people, and Corrientes, which has a population of 268,000.

There is abundant rainfall in the northern part of the region, making it a productive site for growing citrus fruit, tobacco, rice, and forest products. One of the most important

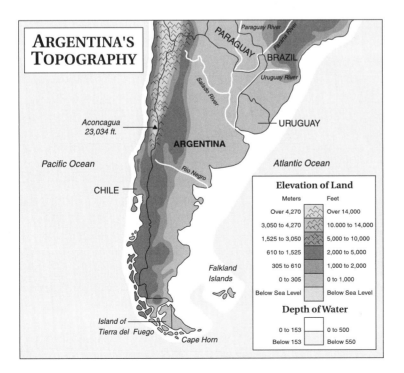

The waterfalls of Igazú Falls are renowned for their power and beauty, drawing many tourists to Argentina's Mesopotamia region.

crops is yerba, which grows in the region's red soil. Its leaves are ground and mixed with water to make yerba maté, a popular drink. Livestock farms can be found in the southern part of the area, where cattle and sheep graze on grasslands.

The region also contains one of the world's most stunning displays of nature's power. Curtains of roaring white water cascade more than two hundred feet before crashing onto the rock below at the Igazú Falls, a horseshoe-shaped series of waterfalls at the tip of the Mesopotamia region at Argentina's border with Brazil. The 275 separate waterfalls, called Cataratas del Igazú in Argentina, tumble over a curve almost two miles long. "The Cataratas del Igazú are one of the wildest wonders of the world, with nature on the rampage in a unique show of sound and fury,"[1] writes Diego Bigongiari in Fodor's *Argentina*. He adds that the water makes unending reverberations as it crashes down, making Niagara Falls seem mild in comparison.

The falls make the region a popular destination for tourists, but the area was fairly isolated until the 1970s, when bridges built over the Uruguay River linked it to the neighboring country and a tunnel dug under the Paraná River connected it with the adjacent Santa Fe province. Improved access to the region boosted its status as a trading crossroads and vacation destination. In addition to viewing the falls, visitors enjoy relaxing on the sandy riverside beaches in towns such as Gúaleguaychú, and gazing at the fifty-foot-tall palm trees in the national park on the east side of the region. In the Corrientes province, a boat trip into the natural reserve marshlands of the Esteros del Ibera, which means "brilliant waters" in the language of the native Guarani people, allows visitors to glimpse long-legged flamingos and brilliant red cardinals, as well as storks, herons, and eagles. There are 368 species of birds living in the region where the Paraná River spills into the marshy wetlands. More than sixty lagoons are separated by masses of floating water lilies, red ferns, and irises. Alligators lurk in the clear water, and other inhabitants include marsh deer and howler monkeys.

THE GRAN CHACO

West of the Mesopotamia region, the lush jungles gradually give way to a much harsher climate that has periods of floods and drought. The flat jungle plains of the Gran Chaco are on the southern edge of a hot region of tropical and subtropical jungle that reaches into Bolivia, Brazil, and Paraguay. The rivers in the Chaco flood each year.

The land in the eastern portion of the Chaco is marshy, with palm groves and savanna. The western part of the Chaco is dry, as the Andes Mountains shield it from moisture coming from the Pacific Ocean. In the northwest is the harsh climate of El Impenetrable, a desert named by Spanish explorers who found it impossible to travel across the area because of a lack of water. The temperature commonly tops 110 degrees Fahrenheit in the dry, hot region where cactus, thorny shrubs, and the white quebracho trees grow.

In spite of its climate, the region produces lumber and is used for raising livestock. The hard-wooded, hollow red quebracho, or axe breaker, grows in the eastern part of the Chaco. It has been harvested for its high-quality wood and also for its resin, which is used in the tanning industry. The scrub land of the western Chaco is suitable for raising cattle, and the landscape is dominated by ranches, or *estancias*.

Lumber and cotton also are produced in the region, and the town of Presidencia Roque Sáenz Peña is nicknamed "the national capital of cotton."

Wildlife is plentiful, even in the driest parts of the Chaco. Armadillos, lizards, jaguars, and colorful blue, yellow, and green butterflies bring life to the desert. In the marshy east, herons, parakeets, parrots, yellow-winged blackbirds,

YERBA MATÉ

The *yerba* that grows in the northeast part of Argentina is used to make a strong tea that is popular with Argentines. *Yerba*, an evergreen of the holly family, needs little rain and low humidity to grow. Branches are cut from the trees in May and September and are dried over wood fires. When the leaves are brittle, they are shaved off and crushed. They are then put in packages and are ready to be sold. Drinking a bitter tea made with *yerba* leaves began with the native Guarani people. They shared the drink with Jesuit missionaries, who began cultivating the plant.

Yerba maté is usually drunk with friends. The yerba maté is put in a wooden cup called a *mate*. Very hot water, and sometimes sugar, is poured over it. It is sipped through a *bombilla*, or metal drinking straw, which has a filter at the bottom. When the gourd is empty, it is refilled with hot water and passed to the next person. In some villages, there are kettles of hot water in public places so people can fill their gourds and make the drink. The drink has become part of Argentina's culture. Sharing yerba maté with friends is a common custom, similar to tea time in England.

Cups of yerba maté, a popular drink in Argentina, are displayed in this photo.

and hawks flit about the rain forest and soar above the swamps. Other animals inhabiting the area include *capybaras*, the world's largest rodent, as well as tapirs, anteaters, and monkeys.

The Andes and Puna

A third of Argentina is covered by the Andes Mountains, a range that stretches down South America's west coast. In northwest Argentina, the Andes's peaks reach nearly twenty-two thousand feet. The mountains divide into subranges with valleys between the towering mountains. The landscape is a study in contrasts, with lush green forests, snow-capped peaks, and barren desert.

The cold, dry Puna to the east of the Andes's peaks is a high-altitude desert that stretches from Argentina into Bolivia. It is windy, stony, and treeless in this region, although grass and shrubs grow in the dry soil. Llamas, alpacas, and guanaco, which look like camels without humps, roam the ravines. Some areas of the Puna are not drained by rivers, and rainwater pools in lakes to form salt flats. East of the Puna are foothills and lowlands, called *valles*. Rain is plentiful in summer in this area and often floods roads. The valleys and foothills of the Andes have a climate that is good for growing grapes and lemons, and this region is the largest producer of lemons in the world. Area farmers also raise livestock and grow sugarcane, olives, and tobacco. The area is rich in mineral resources as well. Tin, lead, zinc, silver, and iron are mined, although the minerals are not as plentiful as the Spaniards had expected.

Tourists experience the beauty of the Andes by taking the Tren a las Nubes, or "Train to the Clouds," leading from Salta to the high altitude of the Puna. The region contains man-made wonders in addition to striking mountain views. The railroad that runs through these mountains, built between 1911 and 1948, includes 21 tunnels, 31 bridges, 13 viaducts, and 1,279 bends.

The Cuyo

The tall peaks of the Andes continue to dominate the Cuyo, the central western portion of Argentina. Aconcagua is the highest peak in the Western hemisphere at twenty-three thousand feet, and other peaks soar to heights of more than twenty-two thousand feet. East of the Andes ranges are valleys, deserts, plains, and smaller mountain ranges. Shielded from wet weather by the Andes Mountains, the region gets little rain but is watered by several rivers.

The rugged mountain area is fertile as well as breathtakingly beautiful. Water to irrigate crops such as olives and melons comes from melting snows in the Andes. Fruit trees grow in the region, and its dry, sunny weather makes it the perfect location to cultivate grapes. The province of Mendoza produces almost three-quarters of the country's wines and is in the heart of this wine district.

The region also has an abundance of fossils. The fifteen thousand-acre Ischigualsto Provincial Park, also called Valley of the Moon, is known for its dinosaur bones, which are found in the red sandstone rock formations and volcanic ash cliffs. Unusual rock formations and a petrified forest make the area even more interesting. Fossils are also found in the Sierra de Las Quijadas National Park in the northwestern part of the San Luis province. This park's features include a natural red rock amphitheater.

These natural areas are home to a variety of wildlife. In the Valley of the Moon, red foxes and pumas live in the bushes that dot the large basin. Cougars, tortoises, gray foxes, and snakes, as well as falcons, eagles, and condors, make their homes amid the scrub grass and quebracho trees of the Sierra de Las Quijadas National Park.

THE PAMPA

While the mountains offer the best place to grow grapes and lemons, the flat land of the Pampa in central Argentina ranks with the best regions in the world for producing grain and raising livestock. A temperate climate, moderate winds, and adequate rain make this region well-suited to agricultural production. The first settlers in Buenos Aires brought cattle and horses to the region. When the first settlement was abandoned, the herds ran wild and roamed the open plains. The animals thrived on the grass of the fertile pampas, and later settlers and Argentine cowboys called gauchos rounded up the cattle and used them for their hides as well as a source of food. The area has now been divided into farms and ranches, or estancias. Farmers cultivate grain and raise beef cattle and herds of dairy cows.

The name "pampa" comes from the native South American Indian word for a flat, featureless expanse of land. Although the plain is broken by ranges of hills in the west, it is mainly flat with few trees and an abundance of grass. Flooding can be a problem on the grasslands, but in general crops grow well in the rich soil.

The Pampa is divided into two sections: the *pampa humeda*, or moist pampa, to the east and the *pampa seca*, or dry pampa, to the west and south. The *pampa humeda* gets almost twice as much rain each year as the *pampa seca*. The northern portion of the moist pampa is best suited for grain production, while cattle farming is more dominant to the east.

The Pampa is Argentina's most densely populated region. More than 23 million people, or 70 percent of Argentina's population, live in this region. Cities grew up in this region to support Argentina's two major industries, grain production and cattle ranching. There are ports for exporting grain and livestock at Rosario, Santa Fe, and Bahía Blanca. The country's major port is in its largest city, Buenos Aires.

A young gaucho drives his herd out to pasture. The flat landscape of the Pampa is well suited for raising livestock.

Buenos Aires sits at the mouth of the Río de la Plata basin. More than one third of Argentina's population reside in this cosmopolitan city.

BUENOS AIRES

Situated on the eastern edge of the Pampa, Buenos Aires is Argentina's capital and dominant city. More than a third of the people in Argentina live in Buenos Aires and nearby towns. Greater Buenos Aires, which includes the country's seat of government, the Federal District, has a population of 13 million.

Buenos Aires is a sophisticated city with a European feel. One travel writer compares it to the capital of France. "Its compact size and regular center is reminiscent of Paris, and its tree-lined avenues and frequent plazas have a beguiling, faded elegance,"[2] says the Lonely Planet World Guide. Its museums, restaurants, tango halls, parks, wide boulevards and European architecture give it an international air.

The city at the mouth of the Río de la Plata basin first grew up as a port, because it is the natural entrance to a river system and the southeastern side of South America. As Argentina's largest city, it is the country's economic center, containing the headquarters of many of the nation's industries as well as the Federal District, comparable to Washington, D.C. The president conducts official business in the

Casa Rosada, or Pink House. The Greater Buenos Aires area, along with the urban areas from San Lorenzo in the northwest to La Plata in the southeast, is known as the Littoral. This manufacturing center contains 70 percent of Argentina's industrial base.

PATAGONIA

The noise, traffic, and colorful neighborhoods of Buenos Aires are in vivid contrast to the emptiness of Patagonia. A cool, dry, windy part of Argentina south of the Río Colorado, Patagonia rises in a grassy plain from the Atlantic Ocean to the Andes Mountains. The country's southernmost region is known mainly for its wildlife, open spaces, and stark beauty.

Patagonia is dominated by glaciers and vast, featureless plains. Grasses, low shrubs, and cactus grow on the plateaus and flat-bottomed canyons, while ice fields and the largest glaciers outside Antarctica cover Glaciers National Park in the southern Andes. The region is barren, vast, and captivating. "Almost everything in Patagonia is on a large scale," writes Charlie Nurse in *Argentina Handbook*. "The traveler will also notice the enormous skies and the

views over long distances which are often particularly beautiful in the early morning and at dusk as the light reflects off the Andean range."[3]

Ocean waves crash against the cliffs along the Atlantic coast. Magellan penguins huddle in their nests on the Peninsula Valdes, which juts into the Atlantic Ocean. Seals, cormorants, gulls, and other varieties of penguins use the coast as a breeding ground. In March and April, black-and-white killer whales can be spotted off the coast, near colonies of sea lions.

The region's lake districts in the Andes foothills offer peaceful, scenic views. Deep blue glacial lakes surrounded by snow-capped mountains and volcanoes, meadows blooming with pink and purple lupine, gurgling glacial streams, and cascading rivers give Patagonia's northern lake district a captivating appearance. In Lanin National Park, which has twenty-four glacial lakes, cougars and wildcats live in forests and groves of pinelike araucaria trees, which are also called monkey puzzle trees. In the Nahuel Huapi National Park, twisted, pale orange trees grow on Victoria Island. Lakes, rivers, and glaciers sparkle at the foot of the park's white-topped mountains. Many visitors stay in San Carlos de Bariloche, a city known for resorts, ski excursions, and delicious chocolate. Although the scenery is breathtaking, the region's winters are cold, with wind and snowstorms.

The southern part of Patagonia is too cold and dry for farmers to grow many crops, but alfalfa, fruits, and vegetables grow on some irrigated land in the Colorado and Negro river valleys. In the south, farmers raise herds of sheep which graze on grass in the canyons as well as on the plateaus and cliff sides. Mineral resources, such as oil, coal, and iron ore, lie under the soil. Most of Argentina's oil comes from Patagonia. Oil was discovered north of the community of Comodora Rivadavia in 1907, and the area now produces a third of the country's oil.

In the far south is the territory of Tierra del Fuego, "land of fire." The name was given to the island by European sailors who passed by the island in the sixteenth century and saw fires lit by the native people now known as the Shelknam Indians. The territory, which is separated from the mainland by the Strait of Magellan, belongs to both Chile and Argentina. Its capital, Ushuaia, is the world's southernmost permanent settlement and is a base for tourists visiting the area or Antarctica.

Argentina also has a claim on some land in Antarctica, 650 miles away. Its claim stems from a decision in the 1490s by Pope Alexander VI which allowed Spain's king to claim land west of the forty-sixth meridian. Since Argentina was ruled by Spain before becoming independent, the South American

✸ THE FALKLAND ISLANDS

The Falklands, called Las Islas Malvinas in Argentina, were claimed at different times by France, Spain, and England. Negotiations gave the islands to England in 1771, but the Spanish remained at a port on the island until 1806. The island was abandoned between 1806 and 1820, resulting in little government regulation in the area and the surrounding

waters, which were abundant with seals.

An Argentine governor appointed in 1820 tried to prevent foreign ships from harvesting seals, but he was ineffective. After revolts by sea captains, a mutiny, and a period of lawlessness, British administration took over and controlled the area, thanks to Britain's strong navy. Argentina tried to assert its claim over the islands with military action in 1982, but Britain responded and maintained its hold on the islands.

Seal hunters capture their prey in the Falkland Islands.

nation claims to own a portion of Antarctica, even though the continent had not yet been discovered when the pope's decision was issued. However, the United States does not recognize all of the Antarctic land claimed by Argentina, or its claim to the Malvinas Islands, which lie about 250 miles to the east of Argentina in the Atlantic Ocean and are also claimed by Great Britain as the Falkland Islands. A few thousand people live on the islands, which have a damp, cool climate. The wind can blow fiercely across the islands, and there are few trees.

A VARIED LANDSCAPE

From the windy, cool Falkland Islands to the lush, colorful jungles of Mesopotamia, Argentina is a land of beauty and desolation. It has some of the tallest mountains and richest soil in the world, as well as extremely harsh environments of desert and ice. It is a country with a varied landscape, from the plains of the Pampa to the snow-covered peaks of the Andes and the barrenness of Patagonia.

The people of Argentina have taken advantage of the natural diversity of their land, using its fertile plains to raise crops and cattle, turning its slopes into productive regions for raising fruit and animals, and preserving its native scenery as areas for recreation and tourism. Argentina's natural resources give it the potential to become a world leader, but its history has been characterized by internal conflicts and political infighting, which for centuries have threatened national stability.

A Tumultuous Beginning

Argentina's history is laced with conflict. From the days of the early tribes through Spanish settlement, and through the achievement of independence and into the twentieth century, the country has had a difficult time establishing itself as a nation with a stable government. From its difficulties with Spanish authority to the coups and political conflicts of modern times, tumult has persisted in this vast South American nation.

Native Tribes

People have lived in what is now Argentina since 15,000 to 10,000 B.C., although the region was not as well populated as other areas of South America. Some of the earliest inhabitants farmed or lived in walled villages, but most were nomadic hunters who chased their prey for days before killing the exhausted animals with spears or bows. They also used a weapon with two or three stones tied to leather thongs which were twirled and thrown around the legs of an animal.

The tribes in northwestern Argentina were conquered by the Inca from the north in 1480. From then on, the people who had once farmed and made pottery worked for the Inca empire. They produced goods, mined silver, and bred pack animals to carry supplies to and goods from mines in what is now modern-day Bolivia. Tribes in the southern part of the country continued to hunt, fish, and make textiles and canoes as they had for centuries. Their way of life changed rapidly, however, after Spanish explorers began visiting the country.

EXPLORERS

The first European to visit the southeastern coast of Argentina was Juan Díaz de Solís of Spain, who entered the Río de la Plata, or river of silver, in 1516. He explored the estuary, but he and his crew were killed by native tribes. In 1520, Ferdinand Magellan sailed south along the coast of Argentina and met the natives in Patagonia.

In the early sixteenth century there were about 750,000 people living in Argentina. They fiercely resisted Spanish efforts to establish a foothold in the country and to control the land and its resources. Sebastian Cabot founded a fort in the area that is now the city of Rosario, but Indians destroyed the settlement in 1529. A few years later, Pedro de Mendoza attempted to build a fort at Buenos Aires, but it was abandoned in 1537, after being occupied for only a year, because of Indian attacks. Explorers had more success in establishing cities in the northwestern part of the country. Santiago del Estero was established in 1553, and Catamarca was settled in 1559.

Argentina's interior towns had more success because Spain favored trade routes that took goods through the western part of the country and then into Bolivia and Peru. Argentina was part of Spain's Viceroyalty of Peru at this time. In order to control the goods that came into and out of the region, Spain wanted all goods to go through Lima, along the Pacific coast. This was done to make sure the taxes on these goods went to Spain. This policy helped those who worked for the Spanish government and the business people in Lima, and encouraged the growth of towns in the northwest. However, it hindered the growth of towns in the east.

SETTLEMENT

Other settlements in the west and northeast were established by Jesuit priests in the seventeenth century. Native South Americans lived in these communities and successfully grew and sold yerba maté. Although the native Indians had a good relationship with the Jesuits, they did not fare well with other newcomers to South America. Many Jesuit missions were attacked by Portuguese slave traders from Brazil, and the natives were often carried off as slaves. Many other natives died of diseases brought by the Europeans, such as smallpox, influenza, and typhus. The native tribes were also killed in battles with the Spanish. Many Diaguitas in the Calchaqui Valley died between 1630 and 1637. After the Spanish prevented them from planting crops, disease and famine crippled the population. More Spanish settlements were established as the strength of the native tribes dwindled.

Spain became more interested in establishing settlements in the eastern part of Argentina after Portugal and Britain began eyeing the region. Spaniards and people from other South American countries controlled by Spain established new cities in Argentina. They wanted to build a trade route from Buenos Aires to Bolivia, and establish a colony before Portugal or Britain moved in. In 1580, Buenos Aires was reestablished by Juan de Garay. The city grew up around the cattle industry. The leaders of Buenos Aires allowed a select number of people to have the right to slaughter cattle, and eventually gave investors the rights to market the cattle that were in designated areas outside the city. The owners of these ranches became wealthy through the sale of cattle hides and tallow.

Ferdinand Magellan explored the coastal areas of Patagonia in 1520.

Less desirable industries also took root. Buenos Aires was hundreds of miles from Lima, Spain's center of government in the region, and it became a center for smuggling goods into and out of the area. Spain's restrictive trade rules made it difficult for the people of Buenos Aires to get the goods they needed through legal channels, so they often resorted to buying goods smuggled into Buenos Aires from other countries. Goods from the interior of the country were smuggled out as well, and Buenos Aires became a center for illegal silver trading. Spain wanted all silver going out of the region to go through the port at Lima in Peru. In this way, it could tax the silver and regulate how much was shipped out. However, some silver mined in the Andes region was smuggled east to Buenos Aires, where merchants from Portugal exchanged the silver for manufactured goods that were in short supply because of Spain's trade rules.

✹ EARLY HISTORY OF BUENOS AIRES

Buenos Aires, the capital of Argentina, was first settled by Spanish nobleman Pedro Mendoza and a group of fifteen hundred people in 1536. He wanted to establish a city from which Spain could conquer the interior of the country, and liked the sandbars and small stream there. He named the city Nuestra Señora de Santa Maria del Buen Aire after the patron saint of sailors, who was said to bless the sailors with fair winds, or *buen aire.* The name was later changed to Buenos Aires.

However, the native tribes, the Querandi, did not appreciate Mendoza's selection of the site for a city. They attacked the settlement and the settlers left the area. Soon after it was established, the settlement was abandoned.

Some of the people who had been living in the Buenos Aires settlement found refuge with friendly tribe members and settled in the native villages. Many of those from Mendoza's settlement traveled north to Paraguay and founded Asunción. Buenos Aires was reestablished in 1580 by a group of sixty Spaniards and *criollos* led by Juan de Garay. Thanks to support from Asunción and other communities that had been founded, Buenos Aires now began to flourish.

Buenos Aires also became a center for slave trading. The slaves worked in cities in the region, or were sold to traders and sent to other countries. The British ships that brought slaves to Buenos Aires also brought manufactured goods to the region.

Spain tried to take a tighter hold on southeastern South America in 1776, when it created the Viceroyalty of Río de la Plata and made Buenos Aires its capital. The region included land that is now Argentina, Uruguay, Paraguay, and southern Bolivia. This move brought more Spanish government officials to Buenos Aires, in order to enforce the laws of Spain. Silver and other trade goods could now legally go through Buenos Aires. However, traders in the city were not used to government oversight. They resented Spanish interference. There was also resentment toward Buenos Aires from merchants and others in the interior who had profited from the trade regulations that made goods go through Lima. Now Buenos Aires was poised to become a prosperous trading center as well. This conflict between the *porteños*, or "people of the port," of Buenos Aires, and the merchants and other workers who lived in the interior would continue for centuries.

Independence

While the people of La Plata began to grumble about Spanish rule, events were taking place in Europe that would have an impact on the timing of Argentina's eventual independence. Spain was preoccupied in fighting against Great Britain and then France. This left few Spanish ships to trade with Buenos Aires, so the *porteños* began trading with other nations. This strengthened Buenos Aires as a commercial center and lessened its dependence on Spain as a trading partner.

Spain's concerns in Europe also meant that the viceroyalty of Río de la Plata was left unprotected. Sensing that Spain's defenses were weak, British soldiers captured Buenos Aires in 1806. The citizens appeared to accept defeat but two months later the *porteños* drove the troops out. They again defended the city from the British in 1807.

In Spain, things were not going well for the monarchy. In an invasion by France's emperor Napoléon Bonaparte, Spain's king was imprisoned and Napoléon's brother, Joseph Bonaparte, was placed upon the Spanish throne. This further eroded the *porteños's* allegiance to Spain. Their victories over the British had given them such a taste for independence that they began to wonder why they were still taking orders from a viceroy who represented the Spanish government. A group of upper-class citizens of Buenos Aires, both those who were from Spain and those of Spanish descent, stripped the viceroy of his power and elected their own officials in 1810. This local declaration of independence paved the way for Argentina to become an independent nation six years later.

However, the bid for independence was not unified. Regional leaders outside Buenos Aires still resented how powerful the city had become, and did not want to be governed by Buenos Aires. Their concerns were often not addressed by leaders in Buenos Aires. The regional leaders wanted to be part of an independent country, but preferred to have a loose confederation or be on equal footing with Buenos Aires rather than be under the control of a strong central government. There were also Spanish forces to be dealt with. Spanish troops from Córdoba were defeated, but the Argentine army also fought in present-day Bolivia and Paraguay. The Argentines lost control over land that is now in those

José de San Martín leads his army over the Andes. San Martín's troops safeguarded Argentina's newfound independence.

countries, as well as present-day Uruguay. However, the independence movement was still strong. José de San Martín, regarded as Argentina's greatest military hero, knew it was important to get Spanish forces out of South America. He led an army over the Andes Mountains and in 1817 and 1818 defeated the Spanish in Chile. He then won victories in Bolivia.

As Spain's forces were weakening, the country that would become Argentina was still wrestling with the question of how the region should be governed. As the country dealt with military problems and a lack of unity, a constitutional congress met at Tucumán in 1816. The United Provinces of the Río de la Plata was declared to be an independent nation, no longer under Spanish rule. Buenos Aires and the interior were united in an uneasy alliance. However, it was unclear how the new nation should be governed.

FROM CHAOS TO CONSTITUTION

Early leadership of the United Provinces of the Río de la Plata was tumultuous, as leaders from Buenos Aires and the interior provinces competed for domination over the country. In the 1820s, the differences between the *unitarios*, who wanted a strong central government, and *federales*, who wanted local power for those in the interior of the country, sometimes escalated into bloodshed. Aggravating the situation, a constitution enacted in 1826 emphasized the interests of Buenos Aires over those of the interior. The citizens of the interior became poorer as the goods that came into the port of Buenos Aires were taxed, giving it a source of income that other areas of the country lacked.

A degree of stability was achieved after Juan Manuel de Rosas, a rich landowner from a powerful colonial family, took office in 1829. He had influence among those in the Buenos Aires province, and also with the gauchos of the west. He promoted a strong army while protecting the church and farming interests.

However, de Rosas also repressed freedom of expression and oversaw a harsh military rule with a spy network and secret police. Men had to wear red ribbons and grow sideburns to show allegiance to him and his government. He also enacted trade restrictions that angered other countries, and in the 1852 Battle of Caseros he faced troops from Uruguay and Brazil as well as his opponents in Argentina. Upon losing the battle, he was obliged to leave office.

Juan Manuel de Rosas was a powerful leader of the United Provinces of the Río de la Plata.

Later in 1852, regional leaders signed the San Nicolás Agreement, which created the Argentine Confederation and supported liberal trade, education, and a strong central government, as well as taking away the economic advantages Buenos Aires had enjoyed. A new constitution was approved in 1853. However, Buenos Aires refused to support this agreement. The nation's new capital was Paraná, and rivalry continued between Buenos Aires and the rest of the nation.

WAR

Between 1853 and 1861, five short civil wars were fought between the province of Buenos Aires and the rest of the country. In 1862, changes were made to the constitution. Buenos Aires agreed to join the nation now called the Argentine Confederation. Argentina was united with the city of Buenos Aires as its capital.

However, the country was still not at peace. Between 1865 and 1870, Argentina joined with Brazil and Uruguay in the War of the Triple Alliance against Paraguay. Following the war, Argentina received some land from Paraguay.

The country's leaders also wanted to take over the remaining lands inhabited by Argentina's native tribes. Presidents Domingo Faustino Sarmiento and Nicolas Avellaneda had little mercy on the Indians living in Argentina, as the Conquest of the Desert virtually annihilated the remaining native peoples between 1879 and 1883. General Julio A. Roca, who had led the start of the campaign, was elected president in 1880. As his recent predecessors had, he encouraged immigrants to move into Patagonia and the Pampa, taking over lands whose original inhabitants had been killed.

IMMIGRATION AND THE GOLDEN AGE

The deaths of many native South Americans left much of Argentina sparsely populated. Argentina encouraged immigration in order to boost its population, settle the lands of the interior, and develop the Pampa. People from Wales, England, Germany, Poland, the Ukraine, and Basque Spain moved into western Argentina. Russian Jews and other immigrants from the Middle East and Italy settled in Buenos Aires. The influx of immigrants from so many places made Argentina more like Europe than other South American countries.

The years between 1880 and 1910 were Argentina's prosperous golden age. Argentina thrived as public works projects helped open the country to trade and settlement. Railroads were built, ports were dredged, and a canal was built at Rosario. The *estancias* of the Pampas produced ample amounts of food and Argentina was able to export grain and cattle products. As its ranching and farming industries generated wealth, Argentina became the sixth-richest nation in the world and seemed poised to become a world power.

However, there was an undercurrent of conflict beneath this prosperous veneer. Leaders often resorted to violence and corrupt practices to get and maintain their positions. Although Argentina was a republic, only adult men could vote and elections were routinely rigged. For example, people who opposed the party in power were kept away from the polls, and many voters did not vote for their true preferences because the secret ballot did not exist. Another cause of popular discontent was the concentration of much of the country's wealth in an elite upper class. The workers resented this, and they began to make their voices heard in the late 1800s. An economic crisis gripped the country in the early 1890s, heightening the people's desire for a change in leadership.

REFORM AND STRUGGLES

Demanding an end to the upper-class domination of Argentina's government, a middle class of merchants, joined by factory workers and tenant farmers, rebelled at the turn of the twentieth century. They wanted a voice in politics, and found it in the Radical Party, led by Hipólito Irigoyen. President Roque Sáenz Peña was elected in 1910, and he favored the reformation of voting laws. In 1912, the Sáenz Peña Law took effect. Only men could vote, and they could now cast a ballot in secret; they were, however, legally required to vote.

Irigoyen was elected president in 1916, giving the middle class the power it had sought. However, the country faced

✳ ARGENTINA'S FLAG

The Argentine flag recalls the sunshine that filtered through the clouds over Buenos Aires on May 25, 1810, when its inhabitants declared independence from Spain. The Sun of May is in the center of the Argentine flag, in the middle of a white stripe. Stripes of light blue, which stand for the color of Argentina's sky, are on the top and bottom of the flag.

A flag with the national colors of blue and white was first flown in Rosario on February 27, 1812. Doña Maria Catherine Echevarría de Viral made the flag, and Manuel Belgrano hoisted it for the first time. The flag was first flown in Buenos Aires that August. The flag was officially adopted by Argentina's government in 1816, and the Sun of May was added in 1818.

economic problems Irigoyen could not solve. World War I (1914–1918) made it risky for European nations to send ships to Argentina. Only goods that were absolutely necessary, such as meat, were purchased from South America. Grain could be purchased elsewhere, and the wheat and corn Argentina used to send to Great Britain and France were left in the fields. When the war ended, demand for Argentine goods rose and Argentina's workers wanted to benefit from the country's economic revival. There were mass protests as workers pushed for better working conditions and higher wages. More than 150,000 protesters took to the streets in Buenos Aires in 1919, paralyzing the city and port, after workers at a steel mill organized a strike. The military was used to control the strikers, attacking them for a week.

Although he claimed to support the middle class, Irigoyen's ideals were corrupted and he gave jobs and government contracts to his supporters. He could not be reelected under the Argentine Constitution, which said that a president could not serve consecutive terms, and he supported Marcelo T. de Alvear to succeed him in office. He thought he could control de Alvear and in effect still rule the country, but de Alvear refused to be Irigoyen's puppet. He tried unsuccessfully to purge the public payroll of superfluous and poorly performing political appointees who had been given jobs by Irigoyen, but Irigoyen was again elected in 1928 and resumed using government money to pay his political allies for work performed occasionally if at all.

During Irigoyen's presidency the country was also suffering from problems due to an agricultural surplus, as an excess supply of grain brought low prices. Farmers and those who transported the crop were hurt in the pocketbook. The government, which had been collecting taxes on imports and exports, was in a financial bind as well. When there was a drop in the sale of trade goods, the government collected less money in taxes. Then, beginning a pattern that would be seen again and again in Argentina, Irigoyen's corrupt, economically disastrous regime was toppled by a military coup in 1930.

NEW LEADERS, OLD PROBLEMS

The removal of Irigoyen as president did not improve things, however. The new leaders were no more honest than

Irigoyen. There were fraudulent and rigged elections under General José F. Uriburu, who had led the coup that ousted Irigoyen, and his successor, Augustín P. Justo. Between 1932 and 1943 Argentina suffered through what has been called the Infamous Decade. Economic difficulties accompanying the worldwide depression prompted leaders to make trade treaties with countries such as Great Britain to keep the economic crisis in check. Under the Plan of Economic Action, established in 1933, an exchange board granted permits to traders. This provided a large profit for the government, and helped the economy. However, it also led to fewer jobs in rural areas, and more people moved to cities. Although the government was aiding the economy, it was still censoring people with opposing views.

Soldiers in Buenos Aires celebrate General José F. Uriburu's victory over Argentine president Hipólito Irigoyen.

Argentina's economy again ran into problems in the 1940s: Thriving factories produced high volumes of goods, but because of World War II, there were not enough ships to carry the products to other nations. The country remained neutral during the first part of World War II, but the United States and other nations suspected Argentines of sympathizing with Germany's Nazi government, although some of the country's influential people were supportive of the Allies, especially Great Britain. The majority of people in Argentina were not sympathetic to the United States, as U.S. tariffs and quarantines had kept Argentina from selling products in U.S. markets. Argentina also feared that U.S. support of other South American nations would lead to military conflicts. Before this issue could be settled, another military coup rocked Argentina's government.

In 1943, the government of Ramón S. Castillo was toppled. General Pedro Ramírez assumed the position of president. The nation tried to build up its own military strength, as the United States aided other countries in the region. Its leaders considered siding with Nazi Germany, which many believed would win the war and have control over Europe. However, an agent sent by Argentina's government to negotiate with Germany was captured by the British in the West Indies. Argentina broke off relations with the Nazis and their allies. The move cost Ramírez his position as president, and his vice president, General Edelmiro Farrell, became the country's leader.

The nation's new vice president was another of the coup leaders, Colonel Juan Domingo Perón, who would have an impact on Argentine politics for rest of the century and beyond. Argentina had emerged from a tumultuous early period to become a leading nation, before corruption and turbulent economic conditions hampered its ability to realize its potential. Perón would seek to better the lives of the people of Argentina. However, the conflict, instability, and corruption that had persisted within its government would continue to plague the country for decades.

Persistent Peronism

3

Argentina in 1943 was a divided country. The workers demanded more rights and a better life, while business owners and upper-class elite wanted to preserve their lifestyle. Neither group cared to do what was best for the country as a whole. This regionalism was a carryover from the time the country was established, when the *porteños* of Buenos Aires quarreled with people living in the interior. Juan Perón, who burst onto the national scene in the course of the coups, claimed to be a supporter of the people, although he also did what he thought would best keep him in power. His promises of a better life, and, later, the charisma of his wife, Eva, so touched the people that he spawned a political movement that lived on for decades after his death in 1974.

Perón in Power

After participating in the takeover of the country as part of a military coup, Perón's first title was director of the National Labor Department. Although not the president, in effect he was the most powerful man in the country because he had gained support from labor union leaders and assumed control over the regulation of union contracts. He also introduced social programs, a paid holiday, and inexpensive housing which brought him support from the general public. Brought into office through the backing of the military, Perón looked to remain in charge by gaining popular support from the country's workers. As the head of the Labor Department, he was called on to solve disagreements between business owners and workers. In order to cultivate the people's favor, he settled strikes in a way that supported workers.

Perón's actions gave him the support of the nation's labor force, but angered other government leaders. They were jealous of his popularity, and a little frightened, too. The country

35

Juan Perón and his wife Eva wave to supporters. Backed by Argentina's working class, Juan Perón was elected president in 1946.

had waited so long before dropping its support of Nazi Germany that with the war over, and the Nazis defeated, the nations that had been part of the Allied forces were hesitant to resume high-volume business with Argentina. Argentines blamed the government for the lukewarm reception they were getting from other nations. Fearing that Perón's popularity would push them out of office, the leaders had Perón removed from his post in the Labor Department, arrested, and put in prison.

However, Perón had an ally who would prove to be the biggest asset to his political career. Eva Maria Duarte, who would become his second wife, organized workers to protest his arrest. They marched on the Casa Rosada, the seat of government. This mass protest got the attention of those in charge, and Perón was freed.

In 1946 Perón was elected to the presidency. His efforts in office were in support of the working class. He set a minimum wage, reduced the length of the work day, and helped workers receive more benefits and vacation days. His wife, lovingly called Evita by the people, played a large role in gaining support for her husband. She championed poor migrant workers, whom she called "the shirtless ones," who came to the cities looking for jobs. She gave them money through the Social Aid Foundation, and she was known for helping hospitals and distributing food and disaster aid to the needy. She became a national celebrity, and was beloved by the people.

Perón's generosity to Argentina's workers came at a price. The country was in debt to other nations. Its economy was also hurt by currency inflation, which meant that prices were rising. As Europe rebuilt after World War II, it needed grains and meat. However, it purchased them from North America instead of Argentina, and the nation suffered. Drought caused more economic problems, and popular support for Perón began to diminish. He had given credibility and hope to the poor, and Eva's powerful position had given women a new level of respect. However, he also craved power and he did not hesitate to put the needs of the masses of workers aside in favor of courting those who could keep him in office. He suppressed freedom of the press, closing down newspapers which opposed his programs or ideas. He also strengthened laws which allowed his political opponents to be arrested.

Although he had been elected democratically, Perón also cultivated the support of his former colleagues in the country's military. In Argentina, military leaders saw it as their duty to protect the people, and in their eyes this sometimes meant taking over the government. Perón himself had benefited from this mindset, but in order to be sure that the military would not be tempted to turn against him, he expanded the power of Argentina's army, navy, and air force. However, when he named his popular wife Eva as his vice president, Perón's support from the military vanished.

In 1949 Argentina's constitution was amended to allow a president to be reelected to consecutive terms. Perón was reelected in 1952 for six years, but in that year his wife died of cancer. Without her by his side, Perón did not have the public support he once had. Perón's popularity dwindled as he could no longer keep his promises. Economic problems reduced revenue from exports, inflation reduced buying power, and there was no longer money for social programs. Perón's strong support of labor union demands had forced corporate management to give many benefits to workers, but these obligations were taken on before the industries

✵ EVITA PERÓN

Eva Duarte de Perón was a powerful force in Argentina and her enduring popularity has evolved to almost cultlike status. Born in poverty in Los Toldos in 1919, she went to Buenos Aires as a teenager and became a popular radio actress. She met Juan Perón when she was twenty-four and he was forty-eight, and greatly contributed to his political success. When he was removed from his government position and thrown in jail, Evita organized a protest by workers that led to his release from prison.

Glamorous, proud, and ambitious, she never forgot her impoverished upbringing and worked to help the "shirtless ones," as she called the working poor. Her charitable foundation gave away sewing machines, cooking pots, and shoes. Evita organized health and welfare programs for the poor, even though she was snubbed by upper-class women who had seen it as their role to help the underprivileged. She campaigned to give women the right to vote, which was granted in 1947. Although she could be cold-hearted toward those who disagreed with her actions, Evita was beloved by the people of Argentina. They showed appreciation to the "Spiritual Leader of Argentina" by flocking to her speeches. After her death at age thirty-three from cancer, half a million people filed past her casket to pay their respects. Thousands wrote to the Vatican and asked that she be made a saint. The former first lady has not been canonized by the Roman Catholic Church, but her face still graces posters in Argentina. Her tomb in the Recoleta Cemetery in Buenos Aires is regularly visited by those who admire what she did for Argentina.

Eva Duarte de Perón grew up in poverty and she never forgot her working-class roots.

were strong enough to support them. Under his leadership, jobs had been created and Argentina had become more self-sufficient, but company profits were used for wages rather than for improvements in manufacturing facilities, research, and development. Argentina was finding it difficult to compete with other countries. These problems led to a swelling of opposition, and in 1955 army forces rebelled, forcing the once-popular president to resign. Perón fled to Spain, and Argentina was thrown into a period of rapid changes in leadership.

PERONISM WITHOUT PERÓN

After Perón left Argentina, leadership revolved between the military and those supporting organized labor. Not one of the country's next eight leaders finished his term in office. All were forced to resign before their term ended. Political freedoms were restricted, and the Peronist party was banned.

None of the governments which followed Perón satisfied the country's workers. They were not experiencing the prosperity they had been promised under Perón, and did not want to settle for less. In an effort to gain the support of the working class, Arturo Frondizi created a new political movement with Perón's supporters, calling it "Peronism without Perón" to get around a ban on the Peronist party which had been put in place during the regime of General Pedro E. Aramburu in 1956. Frondizi was elected in 1958 and tried to boost the nation's economy by tightening trade and financial controls. He supported industries such as oil and steel, and started public housing projects. However, his economic plan did not work perfectly. Inflation increased and production stalled. Dissatisfaction with the way he was running the country led the military to step in once more, seizing power in 1962.

MORE COUPS

Argentina's political situation was fragile. The armed forces broke into factions, each supporting a different leader. In 1963, a new president, Arturo Illia, was elected. He tried to help the economy by raising the minimum wage. Although conditions improved for farmers as production increased and more products were exported, Illia could not satisfy the unions or the military, and in 1966 military officers again took power.

The coalition of military rulers, called the junta, tried to strictly control the country. Congress was dissolved, the constitution was suspended, and the Supreme Court was closed. Political parties were banned.

The junta named General Juan Carlos Onganía as the new president. He was in charge of a rebellious country. Unions went on strike to protest the ban on political activism. Students protested to have their voice heard in politics.

The country's economy was suffering once more. Workers' wages were frozen. Machinery was expensive, and factories found it difficult to modernize their equipment. Onganía tried to revive the stagnant economy, but his supporters in the military lost patience with him. Another junta took over.

GUERRILLA GROUPS

To protest the restrictive government and improve the lives of the poor, upper-class youth began getting involved in political activism in the late 1960s. They followed the tenets of Argentine-born Ernesto "Che" Guevara, who believed that armed, committed activists could get governments to change. There were riots as these guerrilla groups began to challenge the government through violence. Groups such as the Montoneros and the Revolutionary Army of the People used robbery, kidnapping, and killing to further their goals. One of the victims was a former president of Argentina. General Pedro Aramburu, who had assisted in the overthrow of Perón in 1955, was taken from his home and killed. His death in 1970 was blamed on the Montoneros. Three of the Montoneros believed to be involved were killed by police in shoot-outs.

The Tucumán province, in the northwest, was the center of much of this political activity. Far removed from the country's seat of government in Buenos Aires, it had a history of political activism dating back to the meeting of the Constitutional Congress in 1816. The mountainous terrain provided hiding places for the rebels, who wanted to establish a base of power among the poor who lived in the region.

PERÓN RETURNS

In an effort to stabilize the country's political situation, Perón returned from exile in 1973. No other leader could inspire the people toward a common goal the way Perón could. It was

Ernesto "Che" Guevara speaks to a guerrilla fighter. Guerrilla groups resisted Argentina's oppressive government.

hoped he could bring some unity and a degree of stability to the country. His ideals and goals were such a part of Argentina that there was a saying that "if Argentina were an orange, Perón would be the juice."[4]

Perón returned to a country plagued by internal dissension and violence. Many political factions supported his return, but each wanted him to support a particular cause. These groups included the guerrilla fighters and those who opposed them. Perón's influence meant so much in Argentina that the leaders of these factions knew that if he was on their side, they had a good chance of gaining the power they wanted. Rather than hoping Perón would unify the country, they wanted him to support their interests. All the activists were fierce partisans; none were looking to promote their cause through peaceful negotiation and compromise. There was a hint of the violence to come: Fighting broke out, resulting in deaths and injuries, at the airport as Perón arrived.

An election was held immediately, and the expected winner, Perón, tried to take control of the situation, passing new laws against political violence and condemning the tactics of the leftist guerrillas. The economy improved at first, buoyed by hope that the aging hero of earlier decades would somehow lift Argentina out of its troubles. However, Perón was ailing. He would not be able to guide Argentina through its difficulties. The seventy-eight-year-old president died in 1974.

ISABEL PERÓN

After Perón's death his third wife, Isabel, took over as president. Although she was the head of the state in name, in reality military leaders wielded the power. The government used violence in order to stay in power. Beginning in 1974, Isabel Perón's close aide, former police officer José López Rega, began directing the Argentine Anticommunist Alliance, which was also called the Triple A, or AAA. It was sometimes referred to as the Ministry of Death, because its police and military officers assassinated or kidnapped opposing political and union activists and others it believed did not agree with the government. Groups opposing the government became more organized and violent, and a cycle of killing and retaliating with more killing evolved. These frightening events would later be seen as marking the start of the so-called Dirty War.

With no political training, Isabel proved to be an ineffective leader. She could not solve the country's economic difficulties or stop the violence. As she became less and less of an influence in the country, the military became more powerful. In 1975 the army went on the offensive against guerrillas in Tucumán. Neighborhoods where the guerrillas were suspected to be staying were attacked. By 1976, many of the guerrillas had been killed. That year, Isabel Perón was re-

moved from power. She was taken into custody by soldiers and a military government under President Jorge Rafael Videla, formerly a lieutenant general, took over. Isabel was held until 1981, when she left Argentina for Spain.

President Isabel Perón meets with other Argentine leaders. The figurehead of a violent military government, Perón was ousted in 1976.

THE DIRTY WAR

Although violence was already a fact of life in Argentina when Isabel Perón's government was overthrown, the country entered into an even darker period under the new military government. Under the leadership of President Videla and others, the government took the work of the AAA a step further. Building on tactics used by the AAA, it authorized paramilitary units that became known as death squads to violently put down anyone who appeared to question the government, even though the threat of government takeover by terrorists or guerrilla fighters was largely gone. Many of the terrorists had been killed before the military leaders took power. But the government did not stop using violent tactics against the people. It wanted to get the idea of the government overthrow out of the public's mind. To do so, the military leaders imprisoned or killed anyone whom they suspected of supporting ideals that hinted at government dissent.

Very little was needed to make one a suspect. College students who petitioned for paper and pencils were under suspicion. High school students who asked that their bus fare be reduced were tortured and killed. A priest who had tried to bring electricity and running water to a slum neighborhood was beaten and killed. Union activists who worked in a shipyard were blindfolded and shot to death. Union officials, community leaders, student activists, and journalists, as well as housewives, teachers, nuns, and church leaders were taken by government officials to be questioned, tortured, imprisoned, and often killed. Those who were taken were sometimes drugged and dropped into the Río de la Plata from an airplane.

The killings led to an atmosphere of fear and repression. Journalists did not dare write about the killings for fear of being killed themselves. Union workers were afraid to organize protests. Friends and relatives who asked government officials about the fate of their loved ones were told that they had simply "disappeared." Government officials denied that they were holding people as prisoners. Instead, they suggested that the missing persons had gone to another country or into hiding. Those who had the courage to try to get answers from the government about the whereabouts of these *desapareci- dos* could be questioned about their own beliefs, tortured, and killed themselves.

When people last seen in the custody of government officials failed to return home, it was said that they had been "disappeared." During the years of the Dirty War, from 1975 to 1982, at least nine thousand people who had been reported missing never were found. Some human rights groups believe the number is as high as thirty thousand. Argentina's military leaders justified their actions by saying that the brutal measures needed to be taken to protect the nation from terrorists and guerrilla fighters. Videla's government claimed it was suppressing terrorists, but in doing so thousands were kidnapped, many of whom had nothing to do with the violent guerrilla movement.

The Argentine government believed that other countries were willing to overlook its abuse of human rights because of the killings and kidnappings committed by the terrorists, and it continued its abductions and executions long after the threat of government overthrow by terrorists was over. Beginning in 1977, however, after the mothers of those taken, known as the Mothers of the Plaza de Mayo, brought worldwide attention to the fate of their loved ones, human rights groups began to condemn the government's misdeeds. During Jimmy Carter's administration, officials from the United States managed to secure the freedom of some of those being held by the Argentine government.

LAS MALVINAS

The acts Argentina's government committed during the years of the Dirty War were brutal, and they were to cease with the fall of the military regime in 1982. But it was not opposition to government brutality that toppled the military dictatorship. In the end it was a poor economy and an ill-fated attempt to stir up national pride that brought about the downfall of the government of General Leopoldo

✤ THE MOTHERS OF THE PLAZA DE MAYO

Las Madres de la Plaza de Mayo, or the Mothers of the Plaza de Mayo, brought worldwide attention to the plight of the disappeared. In 1977 they began holding weekly marches and rallies in front of the presidential palace in Buenos Aires to try to force government officials to talk to them and tell them what had happened to their loved ones. Their meetings with officials were often frustrating, as officials blamed the disappearances on the work of unknown gangs or suggested that missing young people may have fled the country on their own.

As they demanded to learn the fate of their loved ones, the members of the Mothers of the Plaza de Mayo were also in danger of being taken, tortured, and killed themselves. When they asked officials about their children they could be questioned and harassed. Rallies in the Plaza de Mayo were sometimes forcefully stopped by police. In spite of the danger, *Las Madres* continued to demand answers and asked that the world hold the Argentine leaders accountable for the disappearance of their children.

A mother of the Plaza de Mayo mourns the disappearance of her daughter.

Galtieri. Argentina was in dire economic straits. Unemployment and inflation were high. In order to take the disillusioned public's mind off the poor economy, the government
decided to appeal to the people's sense of patriotism and invade the Falkland Islands.

The islands, called Las Malvinas in Argentina, are in the
Atlantic Ocean about 250 miles off Argentina's southeastern
tip. They are controlled by Great Britain, but Argentina
claimed to own the islands. Argentina's leaders thought
Britain would provide little resistance if the islands were invaded. In April 1982, Argentine forces invaded the Falklands.
It initially captured the islands, but Britain resisted and sent
its military to put down the invasion. After seventy-four days
of fighting, Argentina was defeated. Its only cruiser was
sunk, and there were 1,300 casualties. Britain's casualties
were far lower: 255 people killed, 777 wounded, and none
missing.

Following its defeat in the Falklands, Argentina's military
junta under General Leopoldo Galtieri lost all credibility with
the people and collapsed. Galtieri resigned and was replaced
by another general. The new president, Reynaldo Bignone,
promised to step down in favor of the winner of an election,
to take place before the end of 1983.

REBUILDING

Civilian rule returned after the collapse of Galtieri's government,
and Argentina's leaders faced the difficult task of helping the
nation heal in the aftermath of the Dirty War. It needed to deal
with those responsible for crimes against the people, as well as
rebuild the country's shattered economy. The victor in the 1983
presidential election, Raúl Alfonsín, vowed to investigate and
put on trial those who were responsible for the Dirty War. Mass
graves holding the remains of people executed during the Dirty
War were uncovered. Galtieri and Videla were arrested, and
other army officials were ordered to cooperate with an investi-
gation. The Mothers of the Plaza de Mayo pressed for action
against those who had commanded operations during the Dirty
War. Trials for Galtieri, Videla, and others began in 1985, and
Galtieri and Videla were given jail sentences.

Alfonsín also attempted to deal with the country's economic
problems, and promoted social programs designed to help
people deal with the difficult economic times. Although the

Former president Jorge Rafael Videla is escorted to Argentina's Federal Court to stand trial for crimes committed during the Dirty War.

programs were popular with the public, they made the nation's debt worse. In the mid-1980s, the nation's inflation rate sky-rocketed.

PEACEFUL PASSING OF POWER

Alfonsín tried in vain to restore Argentina's economy. Argentina's currency, the peso, had lost much of its value and in 1985, Alfonsín replaced it with a new denomination, the austral. The nation's economy continued to be sour, however, and this hurt Alfonsín's chances to remain president. In 1989, Carlos Saúl Menem, a member of the Peronist Justicialist Party, was elected president. His election marked the first time in decades that power had passed peacefully from one leader to the next.

The country was far from peaceful, however. Government jobs were cut, and rising unemployment and a loss of buying power led to mobs attacking stores in several cities. To quell the country's economic problems, Menem encouraged foreign trade and Argentina became part of Mercasur, a South American common market, which opened trade with its neighbors Brazil, Paraguay, and Uruguay. He cut government spending and was able to keep inflation under control. He converted Argentina's currency back to the peso, and tied its value to the U.S. dollar, making one peso worth one dollar.

One of the country's biggest changes under Menem, instituted in 1991, was the selling of government-owned businesses to private individuals. The sales had the benefit of bringing money into the government's hands. Because private owners ran the companies more efficiently than the government had, however, the sales meant that some people lost their jobs. Unemployment rose and the gulf between the rich and poor widened. Cuts in government spending also meant there was less money for public programs. The country had an 18.6 percent unemployment rate in 1995, the second highest in the world. There were protests in the interior of the country because of the country's economic condition. The poorer provinces were hit hard by government spending cuts, as the amount of money spent on public programs in the country's interior was reduced.

SCANDALS

Menem began his presidency with strong ideas and hope for Argentina's future, but by his second term his administration was plagued by scandal. There were allegations that government officials had accepted bribes and kickbacks from companies looking to buy government industries when they were put on sale. The woman in charge of the sale of the country's telephone system and steel company was forced to resign after she was charged with skimming cash from the sale contracts. In another

Former Argentine president Carlos Saúl Menem is transferred to home detention in 2001. Menem was found guilty of illegal arms sales.

scandal, Menem was accused of selling arms to Ecuador when it fought against Peru. Menem at first denied the charges, but it later came to light that they were true. Critics said Menem and those in his administration used their power and positions for their own benefit, an allegation that had been made against national leaders many times in Argentina's history. Menem also raised the ire of other leaders in Argentina when he issued decrees to make changes rather than working with legislators to set policies. Nonetheless, in 1995 Menem was elected to a second term.

During this term, the Dirty War again came to the forefront. In 1990 Menem had angered many by pardoning officials who had been found guilty of taking part in the Dirty War. There were protests and new investigations, and in the late 1990s the former military officers were given prison sentences under different charges. Others were prosecuted by Italy and Spain for torturing and killing people from those countries.

DISILLUSIONMENT

Menem was followed in office by Fernando de la Rúa, who was elected in December 1999. However, allegations of vote fixing immediately clouded his administration. His vice president was forced to resign.

De la Rúa tried to fix the ailing economy by introducing austerity measures, or severe cutbacks in services and benefits. They were designed to control debt, but they were not popular with the people of Argentina. People became disillusioned with de la Rúa's leadership when faced with an unemployment rate that topped 20 percent and a continued recession. There were nationwide strikes and demonstrations.

In the midst of the turmoil, de la Rúa limited the amount of money depositors could take from their bank accounts in late 2001. Violent protests and looting followed this order, and thirty people were killed. De la Rúa resigned as the nation was in a state of disarray. His successor, Adolfo Rodriguez Saa, said he would create a million jobs and print more money. He lasted only a few days in office, but was in power long enough to announce that Argentina would not repay billions of dollars it owed to other countries. It became the largest country to ever go into loan default.

Eduardo Duhalde, who had been Menem's vice president, began serving as interim president and tried to get a handle on Argentina's difficult economy in early 2002. He ended the practice of tying the peso's value to that of the U.S. dollar, and although the Argentine currency initially plummeted in value, it had stabilized by the end of the year. Some factories which had closed during the country's economic free-fall were able to open and put people to work, and the lower value of the country's currency brought many visitors from abroad who took advantage of bargain vacation rates. But after decades of borrowing money to keep its economy afloat, the country faces many struggles as it tries to resolve its persistent economic woes. After the peso's value was unlinked from the dollar, inflation skyrocketed. The money Argentines had saved and the amount they earned plummeted in value. The country's poverty level rose, with more than half of its people living in poverty at the beginning of 2003. Its leaders admit that the country faces a long, difficult journey. "Of course, it will take years to get back to where we were before the crisis," said Roberto Lavagna, Argentina's economy minister, "but I would say that we have turned an important corner and are finally on the right path."[5]

The country also faces a leadership crisis. Peronism had survived the Dirty War and its ideals still pervade Argentina's politics, but the Peronist party is fractured as Duhalde, Menem, and others vie for power. Although it has managed to keep violent leadership changes at bay, Argentina is still looking for a strong leader to unify the country and lift its people into another golden age.

Daily Life in Argentina

4

Argentina's people come from a variety of ethnic backgrounds, creating a culture that is different from other Latin American countries. The independent gaucho of the Pampas, the sophisticated *porteños* of Buenos Aires, and the down-to-earth people of the interior provinces are part of a nation which has a culture more closely linked with Europe than those of other Latin American nations. But although their country is a mixture of many different ethnic identities, the nation's people share love of family, a persistent hope for a better life, and a pride in being Argentine.

Culture of Immigrants

Most of the 35 million people of Argentina are the descendants of immigrants from western Europe. Today, about 85 percent of Argentines have European ancestors. The first immigrants were the Spanish, and 40 percent of today's Argentines trace their roots to Spain. In the 1880s Argentina needed people to populate its countryside, and millions moved there from Europe in search of a better life. By 1914, a third of Argentina's population had been born abroad, and 80 percent of the people who lived in the country were immigrants and their children.

Many of these immigrants were from Italy, and today 30 percent of the people in Argentina claim Italian heritage. The section of Buenos Aires called La Boca is home to many people with Italian roots. A number of people also came from Great Britain, as the British helped Argentina develop its railway, telephone, electrical, and gas systems, and British companies provided steamship services. Other immigrants included German, Swiss, and French settlers who established communities on the Chaco. Immigrants from Scotland, Ireland, Wales, and Basque Spain established sheep

51

✸ THE WELSH

Argentina's Welsh settlements in Patagonia's Chubut valley date from the 1860s. The first settlers were a group of 160 people who wanted to create a "little Wales beyond Wales" where they would not be bothered by the English, who had prohibited them from teaching Welsh in their schools. They were poor people, who had lived in mining villages in Wales. Argentina's government gave them land about forty miles from Port Madryn, the port they had arrived at, and a settlement was established. Between 1865 and 1915, about three thousand settlers came to Argentina's Welsh settlements.

The descendants of these immigrants now raise sheep and grow wheat and other crops. The city of Gaiman is known for its tea houses, where cream tea and pie are served. The town holds a Welsh celebration each year and its chapels and cottages give it a distinctly Welsh flavor. The Welsh language is still spoken by some residents, although it is losing favor with the younger generation.

Welsh boys pose with their herd of sheep in Patagonia. Many Welsh of this region are farmers.

farms in Patagonia. Immigrants from Poland and Russia, many of whom were Jewish, also settled in Argentina to escape political and economic hardship in Europe.

Although Argentina's population and culture at first glance can seem overwhelmingly European, the country is also home to people of Asian and Middle Eastern descent, as well as members of native tribes, the descendants of survivors of nineteenth-century campaigns to eliminate the indigenous Indians. Fifteen percent of Argentina's population came from countries outside Europe, such as Japan, Korea, and Syria, are members of indigenous tribes, or are mestizos, people of mixed native and Spanish blood. The small number of natives still living in Argentina live mainly in isolated areas in the Andes, Gran Chaco, Patagonia, and Tierra del Fuego. The cities of the northwest were established by immigrants from other South American countries, and have a culture more closely linked to Latin America than Europe. In colonial days Argentina had a large black population, as Africans were brought to Argentina as slaves. However, the country today has few blacks, and their disappearance is somewhat of a mystery. Intermarriage with other races and heavy casualties during Argentina's wars in the 1800s are two possible reasons for the small number of blacks in Argentina today.

AN URBAN NATION

As immigrants poured into Argentina in the late 1800s, the country's cities grew. Many people settled in Buenos Aires and Córdoba. The country's urban population received another boost during the depressed economy of the 1930s, as displaced farm workers found jobs in the cities. People still come to Buenos Aires and other cities looking for work. Today 80 percent of Argentina's people live in urban areas, with almost 40 percent living in Buenos Aires or its suburbs.

Because so many people live in Buenos Aires, the city tends to dominate the country. The *porteños* of Buenos Aires often look down on those outside the city as unsophisticated. This pretentious attitude has roots that go back to the time of the country's bid for independence, when the people of Buenos Aires prevailed over those who lived in the interior to gain control of the new nation.

Middle-class families in Buenos Aires live in modern apartment buildings or in their own homes. Wealthy people may have a swimming pool and perhaps a second home in the country, which they visit on weekends. Poor residents, often those who have come from the rural areas looking for work, live in shacks in slum areas called *villas miserias*. In the countryside, poorer people live in small homes on farms, or find shelter in dirt-floor homes of straw and mud. Wealthy farmers live in large ranch houses on sprawling *estancias*.

RURAL LIFE

Those who live in rural areas are more traditional and conservative than those who live in the cities. In the countryside, gauchos still herd sheep and cattle, and some farmers use a

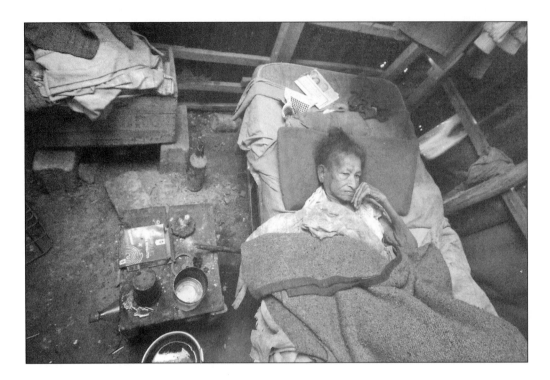

An elderly woman rests in her run-down home. Poverty afflicts many families in both the urban and rural areas of Argentina.

horse-drawn cart to get produce to market. Men dressed in ponchos and sombreros take an afternoon siesta.

Poverty is more pronounced in the rural areas, especially the northwest province of Tucumán. Some families have so little money that they may survive day-to-day on a bowl of soup and a drink of yerba maté. One health services official estimates that 87 percent of Tucumán's children suffer from intestinal parasites, the result of eating contaminated food or drinking contaminated water.

There are also wealthy farmers in the countryside, who live on large *estancias* with sprawling ranch houses. The mansions built by wealthy landowners in the nineteenth and early twentieth centuries may have dozens of bedrooms, formal gardens, sparkling chandeliers, and antique furnishings. Because it is expensive to keep up such large homes, it is becoming increasingly common to rent rooms in these homes to tourists.

IDENTITY

The daily lives of the people of Argentina vary depending on where they live and what type of cultural background they have. Some say that the variety of cultures that make up Argentina has given the nation an identity crisis. Although Argentines look European, the country is part of South America, and being different from both the nations of their forefathers and their Latin American neighbors can be problematic for Argentines. A common saying is that an Argentine is a Spaniard who speaks like an Italian, dresses like the French, and thinks he is British.

The country's people seem to be looking to Europe for the confirmation that they are doing things the right way, and the nation's general mood can strike outsiders as melancholy. Yet at the same time Argentines are exceptionally proud of their country. They support each other, greeting each other with a kiss and warm hug. They go out of their way to be kind, and their helpful and generous acts are known as *gauchadas*.

Argentines like to talk about their country, and Buenos Aires residents enjoy leisurely discussions in cafés over what it means to be Argentine. Many of its people seek to improve their mental health through psychotherapy. They talk to a psychotherapist or psychoanalyst about their thoughts, feelings, and place in the world, often on a weekly basis. The country is reported to have forty thousand psychotherapists, the most per person of any nation.

VARIETIES OF RELIGIOUS PRACTICE

Psychotherapy is such a part of life in Argentina that some call it the national religion. However, Roman Catholicism is the official religion in Argentina and 92 percent of Argentines claim to belong to this denomination. About 2 percent are Protestants, and 2 percent are Jewish. Christians also belong to Armenian, Orthodox, and Ukrainian churches, and there are Muslims and other religious groups. However, less than 20 percent of Argentines attend church regularly.

Popular beliefs that are not part of official church doctrine are a common part of religious life in Argentina. Some native tribe members mix Christianity with their own beliefs, honoring the sun, the moon, and the earth. The dead are often revered, and people make pilgrimages to relatives' graves and the graves of famous people.

Stories of miraculous events have generated large followings. According to one legend, Maria Antonia Deolinda

Correa was traveling across the Argentine desert with her baby in search of her husband, who had been forced to serve as a soldier. Weak and dehydrated, she died of thirst in San Juan. Her baby, however, was found alive and well, nursing at her breast. She was buried in the desert, and gauchos who later found her grave prayed to her for safety for themselves and their cattle. The men and their animals survived, prompting many to say that their prayers had been answered, and the following of "La Difunta [the late] Correa" grew. Travelers ask her for protection, and mothers pray for the safety of their children. Near her grave followers leave crosses and small altars, which may be decorated with license plates, steering wheels, and bottles of water. Shrines contain bridal gowns, engine parts, ponchos, and photographs left by those thanking La Difunta Correa for assistance.

Many pilgrims also visit Luján to honor Argentina's patron saint, the Virgin of Luján. A large church was built in Luján to house a statue of the Virgin Mary. The statue is located in Luján because in 1630 the oxcart carrying it to another destination became stuck. Deciding that this was a sign that the statue should remain in this spot, it was unloaded and a chapel was built. Another famous Argentine statue is in Salta. An image of Jesus on the cross was being carried from Spain to Argentina in the seventeenth century when the ship it was on sank. The statue floated to Peru, and was then carried sixteen hundred miles by horse to Salta. The crucifix was stored in the church's basement for a hundred years, until the city was shaken by an earthquake. After some people heard a voice say that the earthquakes would stop when the crucifix was placed in the church, the crucifix was shown around the city in a parade and placed in the cathedral. A yearly procession with the crucifix commemorates this event. Some say the processions have stopped earthquakes in Salta, but earthquake researchers still list this Andean region as one that feels the rumblings of earthquakes.

Some consider the cult of adoration of Evita Perón a type of Argentinian religion. She is often lovingly referred to as Santa Evita, or Saint Evita, though the Catholic Church has not declared her a candidate for sainthood. Her death is commemorated with songs, speeches, and a moment of silence at the time of her death. Fresh flowers are placed by her tomb each day by those who admire her and what she stood

Devout Catholics wait to enter the church of Saint Cayetano, the patron saint of labor.

for. Prayers and petitions for favors and protection are offered in her name. Years after her death, she is still known around the world. The musical *Evita* and the movie that followed it have captured the interest of a new generation.

As evidenced by the so-called cult of Evita, Argentines see no problem combining government and church affairs. In fact, until the constitution was changed in the mid-1990s, the president and vice president had to be Roman Catholic. Although the practice of religions other than the official religion of the country is allowed, Catholic groups openly play a role in the social welfare of the country, running hospitals and doing social work. People of all faiths are welcome to participate in the activities of Catholic and other religious welfare organizations.

LANGUAGE

Given the many ethnic groups that have influenced Argentina's culture, it should not be surprising that its language is unique. Spanish, the language of the first European explorers to come to Argentina, is the official language of the country. Yet it is not exactly the same type of Spanish that is spoken in Spain or Mexico. Argentine Spanish is called Castellano, and contains many Italian words and local phrases. It comes from the Castilian dialect spoken in mainland Spain, but it has evolved over the years under the influence of Argentina's immigrants and speakers of the country's native languages.

Outside Buenos Aires and the Pampas region, the language includes many words that were used by native tribes. The Spanish spoken by mestizos mixes native Indian words with Spanish ones. In communities with a large population of a specific ethnic group, the language of the homeland is sometimes spoken. German is commonly used in some cities, and Welsh is spoken in some communities in Patagonia, where the descendants of Welsh farmers raise sheep. Many Argentines speak French, Italian, and English as second languages.

The influence of Argentina's many immigrants can also be heard in its slang. *Lunfardo* is a type of urban slang that originated in the early 1900s. This colorful language is influenced by Italian, Portuguese, and other languages. It was first used by criminals as a type of code to keep their activities secret, and its phrases eventually crept into daily use. *Lunfardo* sometimes switches letters around in a word, calling a café a feca, or substitutes a clever word or phrase for a more common term, such as "ball" or "top of a building" for head. A teen whose father acted surprised might say "My old man jumped like boiled milk."[6] *Lunfardo* can be heard in tango lyrics, and is also used by poets and writers seeking to convey the rich layers of Argentina's culture.

CLOTHING

In keeping with a desire to emulate Europe, urban Argentines dress more formally than Americans and closely monitor the latest European fashion trends. Argentines are conscious about how they look, and it is important to them to wear fashionable, well-made clothing. Fur coats and stylish, top-rate leather goods, a product of the country's cattle industry, are not uncommon. High-style, high-priced attire can be purchased in fancy stores and boutiques on the Avenida Santa Fe in Buenos Aires.

Fashion trends in Argentina begin in Buenos Aires and move to the interior provinces. Argentines dress up when going to the city, but in the rural areas clothing is more casual. Loose pants and flat shoes or leather boots are common.

Clothing in the rural areas is influenced by gauchos, the cowboys of Argentina. They wear *bombachas*, loose-fitting pants that tighten below the knee. Around a gaucho's waist is a woven sash with geometric designs in bold colors. Over this is a wide leather belt decorated with silver coins and other silver ornaments. A kerchief is wrapped around the neck, and a vest covers a button-down shirt. Hand-woven ponchos with bold designs and fringes are worn for protection from the cold and wind, and were also used as a blanket when gauchos spent nights on the Pampa. A small beret-like cloth hat or a hat with a wide brim protects gauchos from the sun and wind.

EDUCATION

Argentina's students learn the importance of dress at a young age. They are formally attired when they go to class, wearing the uniforms required by their schools. They generally wear a long, crisp, white jacket over dark pants or a skirt. White shirts and dark ties often complete the outfit.

A solid system of education was established by Domingo Faustino Sarmiento, who was president of Argentina between 1868 and 1874. He based the country's education system on the way the French school system was run. His planning has paid off with a highly literate population. Almost everyone in Argentina knows how to read and write; the country has a literacy rate estimated at more than 96 percent. This is one of the highest literacy rates in South America and is comparable to the U.S. rate of 97 percent.

School is free to the university level, although only children between ages six and fourteen are required to attend school. In addition to the free public schools, there are also private schools which charge tuition. Children attend seven years of elementary school, from March through December. They are taught in Spanish, and can study English, French, and Italian as second languages. They also study math, history, science, art, and geography. Those who go on to high school learn basic subjects for several years before taking

Schoolchildren pose for a photo outside a church. Education is free in Argentina and the country boasts a very high literacy rate.

more specialized classes. After graduation groups of friends may celebrate by taking a trip together.

A small percentage of high school graduates go on to college; about 4 percent of the country's population have a degree from a university. Students who wish to go to college can choose from more than fifty universities in Argentina. The largest is the University of Buenos Aires, with more than one hundred thousand students. The oldest is the University of Córdoba, which was established in 1613. High school graduates can also continue their education at a vocational school.

FAMILY LIFE

Most college students live at home while going to school, as family ties are very important to the people of Argentina. Strong family bonds give a sense of belonging to a people who are very different from other Latin Americans. Family members are loyal and supportive. They help each other get good jobs or admission into a good school.

Grown children usually live at home until they marry, and even then, newlyweds locate near the parents of one or both spouses. Elderly parents who can no longer care for themselves often live with a son or daughter's family rather than in a nursing home. Extended family gatherings with aunts, uncles, and cousins are common for celebrations like birthdays. When a girl turns fifteen her family celebrates the *quinceañera*, marking her transformation from a girl into a young woman. The party may involve a large cake, photos, and a fancy white dress for the young lady.

FOOD

Argentine families typically eat dinner very late at night. The Argentine meal custom is to eat dinner after 9 P.M., often as late as 11 P.M. or midnight, although children usually have a snack at around 5 P.M. and adults observe tea time in the late afternoon. Little is eaten for breakfast, usually croissants and coffee with milk. Lunch is served at about 1 P.M., and people may linger over the meal for hours or just eat a quick sandwich. To compensate for staying up late at night, some Argentines take an afternoon siesta sometime between noon and 4 P.M.

Meat is the staple of the Argentine diet. The gauchos of the pampas survived on a diet of beef and yerba maté, the traditional bitter herbal tea. Today, some people eat meat three times a day. One of the most popular dishes is *asado*, beef roasted or barbecued over an open fire. The meat is hung on a cross-shaped spit in front of the fire or grilled over hot coals. Lamb can also be prepared this way.

Other meat dishes include *churrasco*, a grilled steak, or *bife a caballo*, steak topped with a fried egg. *Carbonada* is a meat stew that combines beef with vegetables such as tomatoes, onions, corn, or squash. It can be baked in a pumpkin shell. Another stew is *carbona crilla*, a thick soup with meat, rice, and potatoes. Potato dumplings, or *noquis*, are sometimes served with meat, as are French fries, bread, and salad tossed with an oil dressing. Meat is sometimes served with or soaked in a sauce called *chimichurri*, which is a blending of oil, vinegar, onion, and spices.

Regional foods in Argentina are influenced by native and European dishes. *Locro*, a traditional stew, includes sausage, beans, potatoes, corn, and other vegetables. Another native food is *chipa*, a small, hard biscuit. Italians introduced pizza, pasta dishes, and an ice cream which is similar to the ice cream served in Italy. The rich chocolate of the Bariloche region was introduced by an Italian immigrant who brought the recipe from Switzerland. *Morcillas*, or blood sausages, are influenced by German and Polish meats. *Puchero* stew, which includes chicken and vegetables, shows the country's Spanish heritage. The tea time custom observed in late afternoon was brought to Argentina by the British. Other foods include *empanadas*, pies with meat or fruit inside, which have their roots in Cornish pastries.

A favorite sweet is *dulce de leche*. A mixture of milk and sugar is beaten and used as a pastry filling or as a topping for ice cream and cakes. It is sometimes eaten with cheese or spread on bread or toast as jam or peanut butter is in the United States. Other desserts include custard cream or fruit salad.

MAKING A LIVING

Argentina is capable of producing its own food supply. Its economy has traditionally been dependent on two industries, agriculture and ranching. Much of its land is suitable for rough grazing, and there are sheep and cattle ranches in the countryside. The country's fertile soil produces an abundance of

GAUCHOS

Surviving in the countryside on a diet of meat and yerba maté, living in small mud huts, and depending on cattle for their livelihood, Argentina's gauchos lived a rugged and independent life. In the 1700s and 1800s, they herded cattle on horseback and worked on the *estancias*, or ranches, of the Pampas. For hunting they used a weapon introduced to them by the native people, the *boleadrora*, which had three stones on a leather strap. The weapon was thrown and wrapped itself around the legs of its prey. Not all gauchos made honest livings; some were cattle rustlers and outlaws, but all shared a desire to be left alone. They enjoyed the freedom that came with living on the sparsely populated Pampas.

The gaucho has become a heroic Argentine figure, like the American cowboy, but was not always so respected. The nineteenth-century president Domingo Sarmiento called the gaucho way of life barbaric and opposed its rebellious nature. The epic poem by José Hernández, "El Gaucho Martín Fierro," changed the country's view of the gaucho in the 1870s, giving the gauchos' difficult lifestyle a more noble slant. The courageous gauchos were now seen as tough and self-reliant.

The gauchos' lives changed in the late 1800s as barbed wire divided the land of the Pampas and cattle no longer roamed freely. Improved roads and railroads took away the need for cattle to be driven to markets. In spite of these changes, the gaucho has survived. Gauchos continue to work on the Pampas, at times riding motorcycles instead of horses, but still taking care of the cattle. Their integrity is celebrated in yearly parades and festivals, and the gaucho spirit remains an honored part of Argentina's culture.

wheat, fruit, cotton, soybeans, sunflower seeds, and ground nuts. Farmers cultivate corn and sugar and also grow grapes, which are used to make wine. Gauchos still work on the Pampa, although today they are as likely to drive a pickup truck as ride a horse. Two-thirds of Argentina's cereal, oilseed, and livestock are produced on the Pampas, and most of the country's wheat crop comes from the Buenos Aires province.

Most of Argentina's people are city-dwellers, however, and while some work in jobs related to agriculture, most work in service-related fields. Those who work in jobs that rely on agriculture may sell Argentina's crops and cattle to other countries. Others work in factories which process food that is sold around the world, or make wool and leather goods. Since the mid-1990s, however, most of the people in Argentina have worked in the service sector. People with these

Many Argentines, like this metal worker, work in factories. Argentina's manufacturing base has faltered in recent years.

jobs work in retail or personal service. They can be nurses, doctors, bankers, store clerks, or government officials.

Argentina also has a manufacturing base. Factories make cars, chemicals, paper, machine tools, and appliances. Petroleum products, iron, and steel are also made in Argentina, and the country produces oil, natural gas, and coal.

Argentina's workers have traditionally been better paid than other workers in Latin America, although the income of the people in the country has been dramatically reduced in recent years by the devaluation of the peso and the scarcity of jobs. Before the value of the peso fell in 2002, some factories were forced to close because they could not compete with lower-priced goods being produced in other countries. Factory owners also lacked the money to update their equipment.

Some companies try to get around government regulations on wages and benefits by hiring workers on the black market. These workers, who are typically immigrants from Bolivia, Peru, Paraguay, and Brazil, receive lower wages, work long hours, and do not get the benefits enjoyed by Argentine citizens. They also do not pay taxes, which hurts the Argentine government. Other people have jobs in another dark aspect of Argentina's economy, the drug trade. Cocaine heading for Europe and the United States sometimes goes through Argentina. The country is also used by criminals to launder money, taking money from illegal businesses and making it appear to be part of a different, legal business's dealings.

Jobs in Argentina are getting harder to come by as the country's economy remains unstable. Argentina has traditionally been a middle-class country, with a large number of people who were neither poor nor very wealthy but were able to live comfortably. Today, the country has more poor people whose focus is day-to-day existence, whose main concern is to find enough food for the next day's meals. Yet its people still harbor the hopes and dreams for a better life that their forebears had for the new country.

5

ARTS AND CULTURE

Argentina's cultural heritage reflects the many nationalities that formed the country. Its culture has been influenced by Europe, as well as Africa and the customs of its native tribes. These blend together in a manner that emphasizes the country's ethnic diversity and European influence to create a culture that is unique to Argentina.

FOLK ARTS

Members of Argentina's native tribes carry on the artistic traditions of their ancestors. Indians in northern Argentina, for example, make warrior masks out of wood. Woodcarvers also make carvings of saints, showing the influence of Jesuit missionaries who lived in the region in the 1700s, as well as carvings of birds, animals, and everyday objects such as ox-carts. Woven goods such as rugs, wall hangings, and hammocks are sold in Santa Maria de Catamarca, and bags woven from plant fibers are made near Tartagal. Pottery painted with geometric and animal designs, jewelry, and yerba maté sets are also made.

Folk art is not as dominant in Argentina as it is in other Latin American cultures. It is concentrated mainly in the northern region of the country, which reflects the influences of neighboring South American countries. The country's relative lack of folk art is also due to the destruction of the native population in the first century of Argentina's history. In Buenos Aires, the arts are more European in style.

PAINTERS

European influence can be seen in the works of painters in Buenos Aires, where art is an integral part of life. The city has more than one hundred art galleries, and outdoor art stalls display the colorful works of local artists. Argentine painters such as Emilio Pettoruti and Xul Solar studied in Paris, and their works reflect the styles and themes they were introduced to in Europe. Many Argentine artists choose international themes and experiment with painting and sculpting in a way that is similar to some artists in the United States.

Yet Argentine painters do not shy away from depicting their country's heritage. The gaucho is one of the most enduring subjects of Argentina's painters. In the early- to mid-1900s, Florencio Molina Campos produced pictures of rural life and gauchos. Raised on his father's ranch, he painted scenes he became familiar with in childhood. His detailed pictures reflect a respect for the hardworking, courageous, and noble lifestyle of the gaucho. Benito Quinquela Martín painted scenes of city life in Buenos Aires, and transformed the La Boca neighborhood into a place for artists. He persuaded business owners to paint their buildings in bright colors. Other popular Argentine artists include Prilidiano Pueyrredón and Carlos Morel.

The gaucho, depicted in this nineteenth-century painting, is one of the most popular subjects of Argentine art.

LITERATURE

The vibrant city of Buenos Aires has also inspired the city's writers. The world-renowned writer Jorge Luis Borges, once the city's poet laureate, captured the *porteños's* pride in Buenos Aires, describing it as "eternal as air and water." Although blind for the last thirty years of his life, Borges had a love of reading, an attribute many Argentines have today. The country has thousands of bookstores, and its printers and publishers produce a multitude of titles each year. The bookstores of Buenos Aires stay open until after midnight, and some are open for twenty-four hours a day. One of the largest events in Buenos Aires each year is the International Book Fair, which brings in more than a million people.

While Borges's works are internationally known, the author who had the most profound impact on Argentina is José Hernández. Hernández lived on cattle ranches as a youth and learned the ways of the gauchos who worked there. His 1872 work "El Gaucho Martín Fierro" glorifies and describes the disappearing gaucho lifestyle. It is Argentina's national poem, and this best-selling classic is one of the most widely distributed works in South America. His work inspired a group of writers in the 1920s called the Martinfierristas, of which Borges was a member. Hernández's work is in contrast to "Facundo," a story written by President Sarmiento which presented gauchos in a much less favorable light. Twentieth-century writers Benito Lynch and Ricardo Güiraldes also used gauchos as a writing theme.

The life of a writer in Argentina has been dangerous at times. Writers Juan Gelman and Antonio Di Benedetto went into exile during the turbulent political times of the 1970s. Jacobo Timerman brought attention to the human rights violations of the Argentine government with his 1981 book *Prisoner Without a Name, Cell Without a Number.* Timerman, a newspaper editor, was brutally beaten. He accused his attackers of beating him because he publicly disagreed with the government regime and because he was Jewish, emphasizing the anti-Semitic undercurrent that ran through some parts of Argentine society, including the country's army.

Other Argentine writers include Adolfo Bioy-Casares, who wrote short stories and novels. His book *Asleep in the Sun* tells of the *porteño* lifestyle. Julío Cortazar wrote idealistic stories, while Ernesto Sabato favored realism. Eduardo Mallea,

JORGE LUIS BORGES

Jorge Luis Borges, a giant in world literature, was born in 1899 in Buenos Aires. His father was a lawyer who dabbled in writing, and his mother translated books. His background reflects the varied cultures of Argentina. He inherited an Italian, Jewish, and English background from his father and Argentine and Uruguayan heritage from his mother.

Borges, whose writing shows both European and Argentine influences, was known for his eloquent use of language and philosophical thoughts and observations on the meaning of life. He developed an early interest in reading and language. His family spoke English and Spanish at home, and he later learned French and Latin. The family lived in Europe when Borges was a teen, and he was educated in Switzerland. After they moved to Spain in 1919, he had his first poem published.

The family returned to Buenos Aires a few years later, and Borges fell in love with the city. His poetry reflected a deep admiration for his hometown. He also wrote essays, and his stories of mystery and fantasy have gained him international acclaim. Some of his works available in English include *Ficciones* (*Fictions*) and *El Aleph*. His vision began to fade in 1927, and although he was blind by age fifty-six he continued writing. He was nominated for the Nobel Prize several times and won Spain's top literary award, the Cervantes Prize. Borges died in 1986.

Manuel Puig, and Osvaldo Soriano are also Argentine authors, as are Marta Lynch, Leopoldo Lugones, Ezequiel Martínez Estrada, Manuel Ugarte, and Alfredo Palacios. Talented Argentine authors, as well as writers from around the world, have had their stories and poems showcased in Victoria Ocampo's magazine *Sur* (*South*).

DANCE

While writers worldwide have had their works published in Argentina, there is one special cultural entity Argentina has introduced to the world. Few things are as iconic a symbol of Argentina as the tango. The dramatic dance performed by embracing couples who glide across the dance floor originated in Argentina in the late 1800s. The people of the working class in Buenos Aires combined elements of the polka with music from Italy, Spain, and Africa into the tango. After becoming popular in the port area of La Boca in Buenos Aires, it gained fame in Paris and other European countries just before World War I. After Europeans gave it their blessing, the upper classes of Argentine society accepted the tango as well. It is now known throughout the world, and is especially popular in Finland and Japan.

Tango music has a lilting style all its own. It has a melancholy feel, and its lyrics are often about sad times or a broken heart. Tango music is primarily performed on the *bandoneon,* which is similar to both an accordion and concertina and was introduced to Argentina by German sailors. Violins, bass, piano, and other instruments can also be used for tango music. Argentine-born Astor Piazzolla, one of the world's best *bandoneon* players, popularized the tango through a sixty-year international career. The most famous tango singer was Carlos Gardel.

The tango is still danced nightly by tango interpreters in restaurants and clubs in Argentina. It is enjoying a resurgence in popularity with a younger crowd, and in 2001 the number of tango clubs in Buenos Aires doubled. Popular tango musicians include Armando Pontier and Osvaldo Pugliese, while well-known singers include Edmundo Rivero and Angel Vargas. Top tango interpreters such as Juan Carlos Copes, Maria Nieves, and Gloria and Rodolfo Dinzel perform the dance today.

In addition to the tango, Argentina has folk dances as well, such as the *zamba, milonga,* and the *chacarera.* Many of these dances originated with the gauchos. In Salta, men dressed as gauchos dance with female folk dancers wearing bold-colored ruffled dresses. Their performances have roots in dances performed by Inca tribe members and Spanish immigrants, and are similar to the dances of Bolivia.

The national ballet is also a source of pride for Argentines. Its best dancers perform at the Colón Opera House in Buenos Aires. Julio Bocca and Maximiliano Guerra became international stars in the 1980s. Bocca is a successful dancer in the United States, and has been in films and on Broadway. He founded Ballet Argentino in 1989 to help young dancers in his home country. Guerra stays busy with an average of 150 performances each year. Young stars Erica and Herman Cornejo and Inaki Urlezaga are ready to follow them into the international spotlight.

MUSIC

Ballet is not the only classical art form popular in Argentina. Opera has a large following as well. Operas have been performed in Buenos Aires since 1825 and today are performed in the Colón Opera House. The stately opera house, called Teatro Colón in Argentina, was built in the early 1900s. Its plush velvet seats, sparkling chandelier, and red and gold trim give performances there an aura of grandeur. One of its most esteemed composers was Alberto Ginastera, who wrote the opera *Bomarzo*.

Argentines also enjoy other musical styles. In addition to tango music, Argentina has folk music that has been influenced by Indian and European rhythms. In the northwest, it is also influenced by neighboring countries. The songs reflecting on love or the beauty of the surrounding countryside are usually sung by one or two people, although the folk group may have up to five members. Mercedes Sosa, a

The Colón Opera House is illuminated at sunset. The opulent theater is home to the national ballet of Argentina.

popular and powerfully emotional folk singer, returned to Argentina from political exile with strong messages of love of country and life in songs such as "Gracias a la Vida" ("Thanks to Life"). Folk songs are traditionally performed with musical instruments such as the accordion, *bandoneon*, guitar, and Indian harp. In Patagonia, folk music is played on the guitar and accompanied by the native percussion instrument called the *kultrún*, a cone-shaped box that is beaten with a stick. Argentina also has rock musicians, including Charly Garcia and Fito Paez.

Concerts in Argentina do not have to be formally staged. In Buenos Aires and nearby regions, *payadores* improvise songs and music. Performers known as *criollo* reciters deliver social commentary through poetry, emphasizing Argentina's Spanish heritage in its folklore.

THEATER

Part of Buenos Aires's reputation as a cultural center comes from its large number of theater offerings. On a typical weekend eighty plays are performed in the city. Bursting with theaters, Corrientes Avenue is called the "Broadway of Buenos Aires." Plays are also performed at a number of outdoor theaters. In the district of La Boca, colorful homes form a backdrop for the onstage action. The country's interest in theater is not limited to Buenos Aires, however. There is also an active theater community in Córdoba, Tucumán, Santa Fe, Rosario, La Plata, and Mendoza.

One of the first plays written in Argentina was *Siripo*, which Manuel de Lavarden wrote in the late 1700s. In the early 1900s, Enrique Garcia Velloso's *Jesus Nazareno* was also popularly received. Today's theater experience also includes dance, music, videos, and even circus performances. Contemporary playwrights provide thought-provoking social commentary. Popular Argentine playwrights include Carlos Gorostiza, Osvaldo Dragun, and Julio Maruicio. Eduardo Rovner's comedy *She Returned One Night* has been well received throughout South America.

THE MEDIA

Argentines enjoy watching their actors perform onscreen as well as onstage. The country produces films that are known around the world. *The Official Story* won the Academy Award in 1986 for best foreign film. It dealt with the problems of the Dirty War and how they impacted the Argentine people.

Censorship was an issue for the Argentine movie industry during the Dirty War. After the country returned to a democratic form of government, filmmakers were free to voice their viewpoints through their works. In 1984, Maria Luisa Bember's *Camila* drew parallels between the 1800s dictatorship of Juan Manuel de Rosas and the military dictatorship that governed the country during the Dirty War. Recent popular filmmakers include Ciro Capellari and Alejandro Agresti.

In addition to home-grown entertainment fare, movies and television shows from Hollywood are also enjoyed in Argentina. Cable television is available, and children can watch cartoon series such as *Dexter, Johnny Bravo*, and *Powerpuff Girls* on Cartoon Network Latin America. Other popular show formats include dramas, game shows, and reality shows. One show called *Pop-stars* followed the creation of an all-girl band. However, people have been canceling cable television subscriptions in light of the country's economic crisis. The nation's troubled economy has also had an impact on television shows produced in Argentina. Stations are buying more foreign material and showing more reruns because they lack the money to produce original shows.

Argentines can learn about the nation's troubled economy through radio and television newscasts or by reading one or more of the many newspapers published in the country. The Argentine media had been hampered by censorship under past governments, and television was used as a propaganda tool by the military dictatorship during the Falklands War. However, today the press has more freedom. The nation's newspapers include the Buenos Aires *Herald, La Nación, Clarín, La Prensa*, and *La Razon. La Capital* is the newspaper in Rosario, and *Diario de los Andes* is read in Mendoza.

SPORTS

One subject that gets plenty of attention from the national press is soccer. Called football in Argentina, the sport is the country's national passion. During important international games, city streets are empty as people stay home to watch their favorite teams play matches in other countries.

Soccer was introduced to Argentina by British sailors in the 1860s and was first embraced by its British citizens. It became

The Argentine soccer team rejoices after winning the World Cup in 1978. Soccer is the country's most popular sport.

a national sport in 1931 and now the entire country seems to have football fever. Children dream of becoming soccer stars and play the game whenever and wherever they can. Games are often going on in fields, plazas, vacant lots, or in the street. People cheer for the national team and choose between local teams such as River Plate and Boca Juniors. Fans are very demonstrative and passionate about their team, to the point of becoming violent.

Fans in Buenos Aires celebrate their team's victories at the Obelisk, a monument in the middle of Avenida Julio. When Argentina won the World Cup in 1986, Argentine fans dressed in the national colors of blue and white swarmed into the streets of major cities to celebrate the victory. Argentina also won the 1979 Junior World Championship and the 1978 World Cup, which it hosted. The country's hosting of the 1978 World Cup was seen by some as a political move and an attempt to distract attention from the human rights abuses of the Dirty War.

Another British game brought to Argentina is polo. The sport is played on horseback, which fit nicely with the gaucho's horse-riding skills. Players on four-member teams swing mallets at balls, trying to get a ball past the other team and into the goal. It was first played in Argentina in the 1800s and is popular with ranch owners, who have the horses and space required for practice. Children hoping to become polo players train on bikes, carrying mallets. Relatives are often on the same team, and some teams are made up entirely of members of a single family. Some of the world's best polo players, including Gonzalo Pieres, come from Argentina.

A game played on horseback that is uniquely Argentine is *pato*. The game involves throwing a multihandled ball through a hoop. It originated in the Argentine countryside and was originally played on a three-mile field with players competing for a duck in a basket or bag. *Pato* is the Spanish word for "duck." Two teams on horseback would try to gain control of the basket and get it back home. The person with the basket had to hold it at arm's length, and people from the other team would try to pull it away. The game was rough and violent, and it was banned by the government at one

❋ DIEGO MARADONA

During the 1986 World Cup soccer tournament in Mexico, Argentina was playing a heated quarterfinal match against England. Diego Armando Maradona put the ball in the goal, a move he later credited to the hand of God. After scoring his famous "Hand of God" goal, he went on to lead his country to the World Cup championship. Maradona's charm and charisma as well as his superior soccer skills made him an international star. He was a passionate player who was not afraid to argue.

The country's most popular soccer star was born on October 30, 1960, in a Villa Fiorito, a poor Buenos Aires slum. He was a small child, so small that the coach of the first team he tried out for wondered if he was old enough to play. But the curly haired boy soon proved that he had more than enough talent to play against opponents who were his age and older. The five-foot-five fireball became a skilled player, wearing the number 10 of a team's top scorer. At his peak he was considered the best soccer player in the world. In 1982 the country tried to keep him from leaving for Europe, but he could earn more money abroad. Maradona played in Italy and Spain, although he also played on Argentina's World Cup teams, and in 1990 led Argentina to a World Cup final. The superstar had a difficult time with drug abuse, and was suspended two times for using illegal drugs. He retired in 1997 and is interested in coaching.

time because of the fights that broke out over it. It was later legalized, although it is now played with a six-handled ball which players throw through a basket.

In addition to producing sports stars who excel at soccer and polo, Argentina is also the home country of one of the most famous auto racers in the world, Juan Manuel Fangio. Fangio won the Grand Prix auto racing championship five times in the 1950s, a dangerous era when race cars were equipped with fewer safety features than they have today. Because he came from a poor family, he learned about cars while working in a garage. He entered his first race in 1929 and upon retiring became president of South America Mercedes-Benz. Fangio, who died in 1995, is remembered for his skill and daring.

Not everyone can experience the excitement of being a top-notch race-car driver, but Argentina's landscape offers plenty of opportunity for other adventure sports. Places for hiking, skiing, mountain climbing, and water sports can be found in Argentina's countryside and mountains. Other sports that enjoy popularity in Argentina are boxing and rugby.

RELIGIOUS FESTIVALS

While some say jokingly that soccer competes with psycho-analysis for the title of Argentina's national religion, the country does not forget its Catholic roots. A number of days are set aside each year for the observance of sacred religious holidays. The Catholic Church has been part of Argentina's culture from the days of the Jesuit missionaries to the present, and many of Argentina's national holidays coincide with important events in the church calendar.

One of the most widely observed holidays is Christmas. December 25 is a public holiday, and the week between Christmas and New Year's Day on January 1 is often observed as a week-long break. Families gather on Christmas Eve to eat special foods, and there are dances and fireworks at midnight. Although Christmas falls in summer in Argentina, Santa Claus is still part of the tradition, warmly dressed in his red suit. New Year's Eve is celebrated with parades. Other religious holidays include the Feast of the Immaculate Conception on December 8 and Epiphany on January 6.

There are week-long festivities traditionally held before the more somber observance of Lent that begins on Ash

A costumed dancer enjoys carnival. Argentines celebrate many religious holidays in a festive way.

Wednesday, about six weeks before Easter. The carnival celebrations include feasts, dancing, and fireworks. From early evening until early in the morning, people dress in flamboyant costumes and dance in the street. They may throw water balloons at each other. In the northern part of the country, native traditions influence the festivities. Floral arrangements symbolizing the stations of the cross are hung in Tilcara's streets. Argentines also trade handicrafts and other goods with people from southern Bolivia at this time of year. During Holy Week, the week before Easter, many Argentines stop work. Maundy Thursday, Good Friday, and Easter Sunday are public holidays in Argentina. People typically attend church on Good Friday and Easter.

Communities throughout Argentina celebrate their own religious festivals. Saint John's Day, June 24, is observed in several towns. The celebration can include adventurous daredevils walking over a bed of hot coals. Parades honor Saint James on July 25 in Salta, Jujuy, and Mendoza. A festival on July 26 in Tilcara is held in honor of Saint Ann. The Fiesta of Our Lady of Luján, the patron saint of Argentina, is celebrated multiple times during the year as pilgrims travel to Luján to pay their respects.

OTHER HOLIDAYS

Argentina's national holidays also celebrate the country's freedom and heritage. In keeping with the historic rivalry between people who live in the Buenos Aires area and those who live in the interior, Argentina celebrates two independence days. On May 25, Argentines celebrate self-government in Buenos Aires with the Anniversary of the Revolution of 1810. An elaborate parade of gauchos, soldiers, and military officers wearing traditional uniforms marches through the streets of Buenos Aires. On July 9, the country celebrates Independence Day, marking the 1816 establishment of the republic.

Other holidays include Malvinas Day, which commemorates the Falklands War, on the Monday closest to June 10. The country celebrates Flag Day on the Monday closest to June 20, the date of the death of General Manuel Belgrano, the person who first hoisted Argentina's flag. Columbus Day is marked on October 12.

On Labor Day, May 1, Argentina honors its workers with parades and parties supported by the country's unions. It honors one of its national heroes on August 17, when the anniversary of the death of General José de San Martín is observed. The people of the Mendoza area also remember San Martín at the end of February when they commemorate his crossing of the Andes to attack the Spanish in Chile. The observance precedes an annual wine festival, honoring the region's main product.

Regional festivals also reflect the ethnic heritage of Argentina's people. In Patagonia events celebrate Welsh singing, music, and poetry. A German Oktoberfest is held in the village of Villa General Belgrano. Folk music that blends Indian and Spanish elements is part of annual celebrations in the northwest part of Argentina.

Other celebrations honor Argentina's unique culture. Gauchos parade through towns to mark Day of the Nation on November 10, while in San Antonio de Areco the gaucho festival lasts a week. Another Argentine staple, the tango, is celebrated with a festival in Rosario del Tala in the first half of January. There is also an international tango festival in Buenos Aires.

The festivals, music, art, dance, and sports that Argentines enjoy embrace the country's multiethnic heritage. Many nations have contributed to Argentina's variety of cultural offerings, just as the tango has introduced Argentine culture to the world. As the nation goes through difficult times, its people find a pride in the cultural ties that hold them together.

Children perform a folk dance at the annual gaucho festival. Young and old participate in these celebrations.

6

CONTEMPORARY CHALLENGES

Argentina's political situation in recent years has been stable, an improvement from the military regimes and turbulent changes in leadership of the country's past. However, the country still faces many challenges, including persistent economic problems, the burden of debt, and corruption in government.

HIGH EXPECTATIONS

Argentina's people are used to a good standard of living. In the mid-1990s, Argentina had the best-paid workers in Latin America. The country has traditionally had a large middle class who lived in nice homes and could afford to eat out at restaurants. They could buy expensive furniture and stylish clothing.

When times got tough, the people looked to the government for help. They demanded social programs to help the poor. If jobs became difficult to come by, they expected the government to create work for people so they could continue to bring home a paycheck.

Argentina's generous social programs and the availability of government jobs helped people in the short term, but also created problems. Politicians created thousands of civil service positions, but this sometimes led to corruption as officials gave high-paying jobs to friends who did little actual work but could not be fired. Problems resulted "because politicians didn't want to tell public employees their salaries had to go down,"[7] said Jorge Stuart Milne, president of Banco Patagonia.

The government's social programs were also poisoned by corruption. Money that had been earmarked for the poor disappeared and politicians could not account for how it was spent. Instead of being used to buy food for the poor, those in charge used it for personal gain. Doctors and nurses trying to save starving children at a hospital in Tucumán, where the number of malnutrition cases doubled in 2002, blamed corrupt politicians for the lack of food in the region. The nation's chief economic officer acknowledged that the country needed to do a better job of getting food to the people who needed it. "Argentina has food for everyone but there is a problem of distribution," said Roberto Lavagna, Argentina's economy minister. "It's incredible Argentina has come to this point. It's a disgrace."[8]

GRIM REALITY

The public often did not see, or did not want to see, the corruption of its leaders. People continued to ask for jobs and public assistance, thinking that this was the way to allow them to continue to maintain a good life. To try and satisfy public demand for jobs and social programs, leaders complied for a time in order to stay in office. This drained the government's

A fifteen-year-old girl holds her undernourished baby. Corrupt social programs have led to rampant malnutrition in rural Argentina.

supply of money. To get more money the government got loans from other countries, loans it has been unable to repay.

Argentina's economy has been in a recession, and the government has not been able to collect enough money in taxes to repay the money it owes to other countries. Lower tax revenues due to the recession mean that the government has less money to spend on social programs, and the poor feel abandoned by the government they voted for. The need to cut spending has also forced the government to cut back on the jobs it creates, a trend that impacts many aspects of life.

The Argentine people are worried that the standard of living they are used to will decline. Once considered a wealthy nation, Argentina's salaries dropped to the lowest in Latin America in 2002. As Argentina's middle-class lifestyle is endangered, some people are giving up on life in Argentina.

❋ WHO WANTS A JOB?

In 2002, the employment situation became so dire in Argentina that one of the most popular television game shows offered a job as its prize. On the weekly television game show *Human Resources*, contestants tried to convince judges that they deserved to get the job that was offered. Thousands lined up outside the television studio when the show scheduled a taping for a chance to be selected for the competition and perhaps come away with a job.

One week the show featured two men who competed for a job as a janitor in a gym. One man was in danger of losing the home he shared with his mother. Another cried when he heard a message from his mother saying she wished she could help him. The show had a happy ending for both men when the gym offered them both jobs. However, for many the situation remains grim. In 2002, people marched in Buenos Aires to demand that the government create jobs and pay unemployment benefits.

Family members applaud a contestant on Human Resources, *a popular game show on which the winner gets a job.*

Doctors, accountants, lawyers, engineers, and skilled laborers who have relatives in other countries are leaving Argentina to find a better life elsewhere.

The gap between rich and poor is increasing. In the late 1970s, less than a tenth of Argentina's population was poor. In 2002, more than half of its population was poor. Health groups estimate that 20 percent of the country's children do not get enough food. Children in the northwest have died of malnutrition. Some people in Buenos Aires and other Argentine cities search through trash at garbage dumps for food or items they can sell or trade. Families of four may try to get by on the equivalent of forty to fifty dollars a month. Argentina used to have barter clubs, where people could trade goods and services. However, now people have few items left to trade. "Argentina used to be all one class," said Leandro Silvera, a university student. "Now there's a distinct upper and lower class."[9]

Children in Argentina have been hit hard by the country's poor economy. Some children in the poor, rural provinces of the north have died of starvation or disease caused by malnutrition. In 2002, one in five children in Argentina was undernourished, according to the Argentine Center of Studies on Children's Nutrition. In some areas, thirty out of one thousand infants die. Although the country produces an abundance of grain, fruits, and vegetables and exports food to other countries, its children are starving.

UNEMPLOYMENT

The increase in the number of poor people has been caused in part by unemployment. In 2002, one out of every five Argentines was out of work. This sharp increase would be disastrous in most developed nations.

Part of the reason for the high unemployment rate is the reduction in the number of government jobs. The Argentine government used to own many industries, such as telephone and oil companies and the railroad. In the 1990s these industries were sold to private companies. These companies often did not need as many workers as the government had used, and many people lost their jobs.

Poor areas of the country that relied heavily on the government for income were pinched when the federal government reduced the amount of money it sent to the provinces.

Neglected infrastructure needed for businesses in the northeast province of Corrientes and other areas hit by poverty made companies reluctant to locate there and bring needed jobs to the regions. This made the people of the areas even more dependent on the government for jobs and income.

Some people have tried to find jobs with so-called black market employers, who avoid government rules on wages and benefits, paying less than the minimum wage and withholding benefits. These workers, who are often immigrants from nearby countries, do not pay taxes, which hurts the government and also reduces the amount the treasury has available for debt payments and programs to help the poor.

Those who do have jobs have found that their wages buy much less than they used to. The Argentine peso used to be worth the same as the U.S. dollar. However, that policy was changed in early 2002, and the peso slid to a quarter of the value of the dollar. People who used to pay ten pesos for food now had to pay forty. Many could not afford new clothes, and found it difficult to buy food.

CRIME

The high unemployment rate has led to an increase in crime. Five times as many kidnappings were reported in the first part of 2002 as in the previous year. People were typically taken for a few hours or days, until their families could come up with cash or an item to trade in ransom to the kidnappers.

Other people resort to theft. One common target is telephone cables. Thieves steal the cables in order to get the copper wire inside. The copper wire is sold to companies who sell it to other countries. Argentina's exports of copper have been increasing, even though the country has few copper mines. The exports have been coming from stolen wires.

People also sometimes turn to violence to act out their frustration over Argentina's economic situation. When Argentina's leaders put a limit on the amount of money citizens could withdraw from bank accounts, mobs of people who wanted their money attacked the banks.

Some people blame the rise in the crime rate on the government's inability to function properly rather than the people's need for money. The weak government cannot control the criminals, who see an opportunity to strike with little chance of being severely punished. "The rise in crime rates is

less economic and more a function of political and institutional breakdown in Argentina,"[10] says Joseph S. Tulchin, a Latin American Program director in Washington D.C.

A tourist leaves a shop that does not accept Argentine money.

DEBT

Many of Argentina's problems are centered around the large amount of money it owes to other countries. For many years Argentina's government borrowed money from other countries, accumulating a foreign debt of $141 billion by the end of 2001. When it did not repay most of the money, other countries refused to give it any more loans.

Argentina's banking system is also in trouble. The peso's value is unstable, and people are worried that it will be worth little. To compensate, some businesses and provinces are printing their own currency. People are spending *creditos* and *patacones* instead of pesos.

SELFISH INTERESTS

In the face of the country's many problems, Argentina's leaders have reacted erratically. They often look to do what would benefit themselves and their own area of the country rather than trying to help the country as a whole. This way of thinking dates back to the country's early history, when Buenos Aires and the provinces in the interior of the country repeatedly battled for control of the country. Leaders from Buenos Aires, the center of the majority of the country's population, want to make decisions that will benefit the city and its leaders. Those in outlying areas believe that their needs, and the needs of the poor who live there, should come first. Neither wants to look at the country as a single entity. This selfish attitude has caused shifts in power, with one region for a time gaining control, power, and the monetary benefits that come with it, only to see the pendulum swing back in the other direction before any real strides can be made.

This persistent division was evident in the midst of the country's 2002 economic crisis, when politicians busied themselves with trying to keep those with opposing views out of office, rather than working with them to keep the nation from slipping further into poverty. The president at the time, Eduardo Duhalde, tried to change election rules so former president Carlo Saúl Menem could not be reelected. He also encouraged the country's Congress to impeach several members of the Supreme Court. This angered the justices, who struck down some of Duhalde's economic policies. As Argentina's government leaders were preoccupied with political wrangling, the once-wealthy country was becoming one of the poorest nations in the world.

CORRUPTION

Argentina's dire economic situation is partly the result of its leaders' inability to resist favoring specific interests for personal gain. Although Argentina's political situation has stabilized and government leadership now changes peacefully rather than by military overthrow, Argentina still is plagued by government corruption. The country's recent leadership has been tainted by charges of bribery, and there are questions about whether the funds loaned to Argentina by other nations were used properly. Misuse of social welfare funds, the inability of politicians to agree on any solution, and political infighting have caused the country to stay mired in its troubles. A currently popular phrase among people in Argentina is, "All the politicians out."

To resolve its problems and revive the hope of receiving help from other countries in terms of loans, other nations expect Argentina's provinces to work together to hold down spending and wisely use the resources they have. Argentina must come up with a banking system that encourages people to save money. To improve its economy, the United States and the International Monetary Fund want Argentina's government to spend less and cut jobs. However, that angers Argentine citizens who are used to government jobs and social programs.

AN UNEASY HOPE FOR THE FUTURE

Argentina's troubles could be overcome through wise leadership and a cohesive plan to move the country forward. Argentina has abundant natural resources, but its leaders have yet to agree on how to use them for the good of the nation. Argentines know their country has the potential to use its plentiful resources, but individual interests often take precedence over decisions that would benefit the entire country.

❋ A TOURISM BOOM

Argentina used to be seen as a pricey country for tourists. However, that changed when its currency was devalued in 2002. Argentina experienced a dramatic increase in the number of tourists visiting the country as people realized that its devalued currency made it a vacation bargain.

The devaluation of Argentina's peso meant that prices went up for the people who lived there. But it also meant that currency from other countries could buy more. After the value of the peso dropped dramatically, a tourist from the United States visiting Argentina in late 2002 could get a steak dinner at a Buenos Aires restaurant for four dollars. A night at a budget hotel, including breakfast the next day, cost twenty dollars. An afternoon tour of Buenos Aires was priced at six dollars.

These prices drew visitors from neighboring Chile and Brazil, as well as Mexico, the United States, and Europe. Three million people visited Argentina in 2002, 15.4 percent more than came to the country in 2001. The increase was most dramatic at the end of the year, when 40 percent more people chose Argentina as a vacation destination. The visitors relaxed on beaches near Mar del Plata, gazed at the spectacular Igazú Falls, and visited the mountains in Córdoba. They fished and trekked in Patagonia, and sampled the culture of Buenos Aires. Tourism has become a welcome source of income and jobs in a country where unemployment and poverty have been on the rise.

Some things in Argentina have gotten better. For two decades now, people have not had to live in fear of violent reprisal from a military government for expressing their political viewpoints. And since mid-2002, the lower value of Argentina's currency has meant that its farmers are finding more foreign markets for their goods. Groups of Argentines have banded together to survive the difficult times, growing food in community gardens and opening neighborhood banks.

The sale of government industries to private businesses has been painful in terms of job loss, but the privatized companies operate more efficiently. Roads built by private companies are in better condition than government roads, which are not repaired. Electrical blackouts used to be common, but now that the electricity is provided by a private utility company, the blackouts have ended. The city parks are cleaner, and telephone service is better. Before the telephone industry was privatized, it could take fifteen years to get a new phone line.

Some companies that had been closed have reopened as the devalued Argentine currency makes their products more competitive with those produced in other countries. The country's top economic official is cautiously optimistic. "Of course it will take years to get back to where we were before the crisis," said Lavagna, "but I would say that we have turned an important corner and are finally on the right path."[11]

Argentina is a beautiful country with a landscape of vast and varied resources. Persistent division between leaders from Buenos Aires and those from the interior has traditionally made it difficult for the country to form a cohesive plan for improvement. Its people are dealing with a difficult time in their history, but this is not the first time they have faced a crisis. There is now reason to hope that Argentina's citizens and leaders are ready to face the current challenges and work together to overcome them. The country's leaders have recognized the need to concentrate on properly using Argentina's vast resources for the good of all as this once wealthy nation of virtually unlimited potential faces an uncertain future.

FACTS ABOUT ARGENTINA

GOVERNMENT

Country name: The Argentine Republic

Government type: Republic

Capital: Buenos Aires (population 3 million in the city, 13 million in the metropolitan area)

Administrative divisions: 23 provinces and one autonomous federal capital district

Date of independence: July 9, 1816

Executive branch:

President: elected by popular vote to 4-year term

Cabinet: appointed by president

Legislative branch: Bicameral congress; 72-member Senate, 257-member Chamber of Deputies

Judicial branch: Supreme Court, federal and provincial trial courts; Supreme Court members appointed by the president with the consent of the Senate

GEOGRAPHY

Area: 1.1 million square miles (2.8 million square kilometers)

Bordering countries: Bolivia, Paraguay, Brazil, Uruguay, Chile

Climate: Ranges from subtropical in the north to arid and extreme cold in the far south near the Antarctic Circle

Terrain: Andes Mountains and foothills in the west, including Aconcagua, the highest peak in the Western Hemisphere at 23,034 feet (7,021 meters); the rest of the country is lowland, with the central region characterized by vast grassy plains, or pampas

Elevation extremes:

Lowest point: Salinas Chicas, -40 meters (on Peninsula Valdes)

Highest point: Cerro Aconcagua (7,021 meters)

Natural resources: Lead, zinc, tin, copper, iron, manganese, oil, uranium; also fertile plains, or pampas

Land use:

Arable land: 9%

Permanent crops: 1%

Other: 90%

Natural hazards: San Miguel de Tucumán and Mendoza areas in the Andes are subject to earthquakes; violent windstorms called *pamperos* can strike on the Pampas and in the northeast; heavy flooding can occur on the Chaco.

Environmental issues: Deforestation, soil degradation, desertification, air pollution, and water pollution. These environmental problems, both urban and rural, are typical of an industrializing economy. Argentina is a world leader in setting voluntary greenhouse gas targets.

PEOPLE

Population (2001): 36.02 million

Age structure (2002 est.):

0–14 years: 26.3%

15–64 years: 63.2%

65+ years: 10.5%

Population growth rate (2002 est.): 1.13 %

Birth rate (2002 est.): 18.23 births/1,000 population

Death rate (2002 est.): 7.57 deaths/1,000 population

Infant mortality rate (2002 est.): 17.2 deaths/1,000 live births

Life expectancy at birth: 75.48 years

Total fertility rate (2002 est.): 2.41 children born/woman

Ethnic Groups:

European: 85%

Mestizo, Amerindian, or other nonwhite groups: 15%

Religion:

Roman Catholic: 92%

Protestant: 2%

Jewish: 2%

Other: 4%

Official language: Spanish

Literacy: 97%

Workforce:

Industry and commerce: 36%

Agriculture: 19%

Transport and communications: 6%

Other: 39%

ECONOMY (2001 UNLESS OTHERWISE NOTED)

Gross domestic product (GDP): $453 billion

GDP growth rate: -4.6%

GDP per capita: $12,000

Population below poverty line: 37%

Inflation rate (2002): 41%

Labor force (1999): 15 million

Unemployment rate (year-end 2001): 25%

Budget:

    Revenues (2000 est.): $44 billion

    Expenditures (2000 est.): $48 billion

Industries: Food processing, oil refining, machinery and equipment, textiles, chemicals and petrochemicals

Agricultural products: Grains, oilseeds and by-products, livestock products

Exports: $26.6 billion (grains, meats, oilseeds, manufactured products)

Imports: $20.3 billion (machinery, vehicles and transport products, chemicals)

Currency: peso (3.26 pesos per U.S. dollar in January 2003. Abandoned fixed rate pegged to U.S. dollar in January 2002)

NOTES

CHAPTER 1: A DIVERSE LANDSCAPE

1. Quoted in *Fodor's Argentina*. New York: Fodor's Travel Publications, 2002, p. 126.

2. Lonely Planet World Guide, www.lonelyplanet.com.

3. Charlie Nurse, *Argentina Handbook*. Bath, England: Footprint Handbooks Ltd, 2002, p. 405.

CHAPTER 3: PERSISTENT PERONISM

4. Joseph Page, *Perón*. New York: Random House, 1983, p. 502.

5. *Washington Post*, "Signs of Recovery," December 1, 2002, www.newsday.com.

CHAPTER 4: DAILY LIFE IN ARGENTINA

6. Cyndy Hall, "Mind Your Manners," *Faces: People, Places, and Cultures*. April 2000, p. 22.

CHAPTER 6: CONTEMPORARY CHALLENGES

7. Quoted in James Cox, "Abandoned Argentina Left to Dance Alone," *USA Today*, September 4, 2002.

8. Quoted in Alistair Scrutton, "Starving Children Haunt Argentines as Crisis Deepens," Reuters Foundation Alertnet, December 2, 2002. www.alertnet.org.

9. Quoted in Jill Martin, "Cash Crisis Opens Class Divide in Argentina," August 15, 2002. www.cnn.com.

10. Quoted in Associated Press, "Kidnappings a Booming Business in Argentina," *The Star Online*, November 8, 2002. http://thestar.com.

11. Quoted in *Washington Post,* "Argentine Economy Making a Slow Rebound," December 1, 2002. www.newsday.com.

CHRONOLOGY

15000 B.C.
Area comprising present-day Argentina is inhabited by nomadic people.

5000 B.C.
Some people begin to build settlements.

A.D. 1480
Inca armies conquer the northwestern part of the region.

1516
Juan Díaz de Solís and his Spanish expedition enter the Río de la Plata and claim the area for Spain.

1520
Magellan explores Patagonia's coast.

1536
Pedro de Mendoza establishes a settlement at Buenos Aires although it is soon abandoned.

1553
Santiago del Estero is reestablished by Spanish settlers. It is the first permanent town in Argentina.

1573
Córdoba and Santa Fe are established.

1580
Buenos Aires is reestablished by Juan de Garay's expedition.

1610
The first Jesuit mission is established.

1767
Jesuits are expelled from Spain's colonies.

1776
The Viceroyalty of the Río de la Plata is established with Buenos Aires as its capital.

1806
The British invade Buenos Aires. Forces led by Santiago Liniers make them surrender.

1807
The British attempt another invasion of Buenos Aires but are defeated.

1810
Buenos Aires declares independence.

1811
Buenos Aires loses land in present-day Paraguay, Bolivia, and Uruguay.

1816
Independence of the United Provinces of the Río de la Plata is declared at Tucumán.

1829
Juan Manuel de Rosas takes control of the government.

1845–1848
Problems with France and England lead to a naval blockade of Buenos Aires.

1852
Rosas's dictatorship ends after his army is defeated. The Argentine Confederation is created with the San Nicolás Agreement.

1853
Argentina's constitution is approved.

1853–1861
Conflict between Buenos Aires and the provinces.

1862
Buenos Aires agrees to join the Argentine Confederation and the city is declared its capital.

1865–1870
Argentina joins Brazil and Uruguay in a war against Paraguay in the War of the Triple Alliance.

1879–1883
The Conquest of the Desert decimates Argentina's native population.

1880
Argentina's golden age begins. Railroads are built, the meat packing industry expands, and wheat is shipped to Europe.

1890
Argentina's golden age is tainted as economic problems emerge.

1912
Changes in election laws mandate secret ballots. All males are required to vote.

1916
Hipólito Irigoyen wins the presidential election.

1919
Conflicts between protesting workers and the army turn bloody.

1930
Argentina's economy suffers in a worldwide depression. Irigoyen's government is overthrown by a military coup.

1932
The Infamous Decade begins. Argentina is troubled by government fraud and violence.

1943
A military coup topples president Ramón S. Castillo.

1946
Juan D. Perón is elected president.

1947
Perón's wife, Eva, champions women's right to vote, which is granted by the government.

1952
Perón is reelected. Eva Perón dies of cancer.

1955
Perón is overthrown by a military coup and flees the country. General Pedro Aramburu leads the country.

1958
Arturo Frondizi is elected president.

1962
Frondizi is overthrown by a military coup.

1963
Arturo Illia is elected president.

1966
Illia is overthrown by a military coup. General Juan Carlos Onganía becomes president.

1968–1969
Riots and protests take place.

1970
A guerrilla group kills former President Pedro Aramburu. Violence and economic problems increase.

1973
Perón returns to Argentina. He is elected president.

1974
Perón dies, and his third wife, Maria Estela (Isabel) Martínez de Perón succeeds him as president; government police squads are formed to crush those opposed to the government, beginning the Dirty War, which led to the disappearance and death of thousands.

1976
Isabel Perón is forced from office by the military. Lieutenant General Jorge Videla becomes president.

1977
The Mothers of the Plaza de Mayo begin protesting the dictatorship and asking for information about the disappearance of their loved ones.

1978
Argentina's soccer team wins the World Cup.

1982
Argentina suffers from economic problems. President Leopoldo Galtieri attempts to build a sense of nationalism by invading the Falkland Islands, which are controlled by

the British. Argentina is defeated in the brief war. Galtieri resigns and General Reynaldo Benito Antonio Bignone takes over as president.

1983
Raúl Alfonsín is elected president.

1989
Argentina's economy worsens, and Carlos Saúl Menem is chosen as the country's president.

1991
Menem attempts to revive the nation's economy by putting national industries into private hands and returning to the peso as the nation's monetary unit, after a six-year experiment with the austral, another monetary unit, was declared a failure.

1995
Despite allegations of corruption tied to his administration, Menem is elected to a second term in office.

1999
Fernando de la Rúa is elected president.

2001
De la Rúa resigns as deteriorating economic conditions lead to violence. New president Adolfo Rodriguez Saa says Argentina will not repay a substantial loan it owes to other countries. Saa resigns.

2002
Eduardo Duhalde is elected president by a legislative assembly. Argentina suffers from severe economic problems. Duhalde attempts to help the country by unpegging the peso's value from the dollar. Inflation skyrockets, and Argentina's poverty level rises.

GLOSSARY

bandoneon: A musical instrument related to the accordion. It is commonly used for tango music.

Castellano: The version of the Spanish language spoken in Argentina. It is influenced by Italian and other languages.

Criollo: A person born in Latin America whose ancestors are Spanish.

Dirty War: The name given to the brutal activities carried out by the dictatorship which ruled Argentina in the late 1970s and early 1980s.

estancias: Large ranches on the Pampas.

interior: A term used by residents of Buenos Aires to refer to the rest of the country.

gaucho: A cowboy who lives on the Pampas, working with cattle.

gauchada: An act of kindness.

guerrilla: A small, independent paramilitary force.

lunfardo: Slang often used in tango songs.

mestizo: A person whose ancestors are both Indian and European.

Pampas: Flat, grassy plains in central Argentina.

Peronism: Nationalistic political ideals based on those of Juan Perón.

porteños: Those who live in the city of Buenos Aires.

quebracho: A tree with very hard wood that grows in Argentina's Chaco region.

recession: A decline in a nation's economy.

yerba maté: A strong tea made with dried and crushed leaves of the yerba plant. The tea is made in a gourd or maté and sipped through a metal straw.

FOR FURTHER READING

Fiona Adams, *Culture Shock! Argentina*. Portland, OR: Graphic Arts Center, 2000. A feisty travelogue that gives the reader insights into Argentina's people and their attitudes.

John DeChancie, *Juan Perón*. New York: Chelsea House, 1987. A look at the life of the former president of Argentina who made a lasting impact on the country.

Lowell Dingus and Luis Chiappe, *The Tiniest Giants: Discovering Dinosaur Eggs*. New York: Random House, 1999. A nonfiction book describing the search for dinosaur eggs in Patagonia.

Ethel Caro Gofen and Leslie Jermyn, *Argentina*. New York: Benchmark, 2002. Argentina is explored with an emphasis on the impact of the country's cultural aspects such as language, the arts, festivals, and religion.

Martin Hintz, *Argentina*. Chicago: Childrens Press, 1998. Argentina's history and culture.

Daniel K. Lewis, *The History of Argentina*. Westport, CT: Greenwood Press, 2001. A comprehensive look at Argentina's history. The author pays close attention to the country's political factions and economic conditions.

WORKS CONSULTED

BOOKS

Fodor's Argentina, 2nd ed. New York: Fodor's Travel Publications, 2002. Where to go, what to see and do in Argentina.

Martin Edwin Andersen, *Dossier Secreto: Argentina's* Desaparecidos *and the Myth of the Dirty War.* Boulder, CO: Westview Press, 1993. Details of the events leading up to the Dirty War, the war itself and its aftermath.

Lucy Davies and Mo Fini, *Arts & Crafts of South America.* San Francisco: Chronicle Books, 1995. Descriptions and photos of the lives and work of the folk artists of South America.

David William Foster, Melissa Fitch Lockhart, Darrell B. Lockhart, *Culture and Customs of Argentina.* Westport, CT: Greenwood Press. 1998. A look at Argentina's religion, social customs, literature, and other cultural aspects with special emphasis on the people who influenced the country's culture.

Alex Huber, *We Live in Argentina.* New York: Bookwright Press, 1984. A look at Argentina's culture as related in first-person accounts.

Charlie Nurse, *Argentina Handbook.* Bath, England: Footprint Handbooks, 2000. A detailed look at Argentina's cities and regions, with sidebars and anecdotes on the country's lesser known features.

Joseph Page, *Perón.* New York: Random House, 1983. A comprehensive biography of the life and politics of Juan Perón, including information on his wife, Eva.

James D. Rudolph, ed., *Argentina: A Country Study.* Washington, DC: Library of Congress, Federal Research Division, 1985. Part of a series of country studies, the book gives background material on Argentina's history.

PERIODICALS

Jayne Clark, "Cheap, Cheap, Cheap," *USA Today*, January 10, 2003.

James Cox, "Abandoned Argentina Left to Dance Alone," *USA Today*, September 4, 2002.

Charles Gaines, "Pampered in the Pampas," *Town & Country*, June 1997.

Cyndy Hall, "Mind Your Manners," *Faces: People, Places, and Cultures*, April 2000, p. 22.

WEBSITES

CIA: The World Factbook 2002 (www.cia.gov). Updated information and statistics on Argentina.

Department of State Foreign Affairs Network (www.state.gov). Official U.S. foreign policy information and country facts.

Lonely Planet World Guide (www.lonelyplanet.com). Argentina's history, geography and customs, as well as current travel information.

The Southernmost South (www.surdelsur.com). Detailed inside information about Argentina's culture.

INTERNET SOURCES

Associated Press, "Kidnappings a Booming Business in Argentina," *The Star Online*, November 8, 2002. http://thestar.com.

Associated Press, "Saa Leads in Argentine Election Polls," ABC News.com, 2002. abcnews.com.

CNN, "Argentina's Dictatorship Believed U.S. Willing to Overlook Crackdown," www.CNN.com, August 22, 2002. www.cnn.com.

Jill Martin, "Cash Crisis Opens Class Divide in Argentina," CNN.com, August 15, 2002. www.cnn.com.

Lucia Newman, "'Survivor' Argentine Style: Who Wants a Job?" CNN.com, September 4, 2002. www.cnn.com.

Leandro Prada, "Starving Children in Once-Rich Argentina," United Press International, November 18, 2002. www.upi.com.

Bill Rodgers, "Argentina Suffers Through Deepest Economic Depression in 100 Years," voanews, November 19, 2002. www.voanews.com.

Reuters, "Argentina Sees Tourism Revs Jump Due to Devaluation," December 23, 2002. www.forbes.com.

Alistair Scrutton, "Starving Children Haunt Argentines as Crisis Deepens," Reuters Foundation Alertnet, December 2, 2002. www.alertnet.org.

Washington Post, "Argentine Economy Making a Slow Rebound," Newsday.com, December 1, 2002. www.newsday.com.

Washington Post, "Signs of Recovery," December 1, 2002. www.newsday.com.

INDEX

agriculture, 11–12, 15, 16, 17, 62–63
Alfonsín, Raúl, 46–47
Alvear, Marcelo T. de, 32
Andes Mountains, 10, 15
Antarctica, 21–22
Aramburu, Pedro E., 39, 40
areas. *See specific regions/region types*
Argentina
  border countries of, 10
  capital of, 18–19
  cities of, 17
  diversity of, 10, 22
  flag of, 31
  geography of, 10–22
  government center of, 18–19
  language of, 58–59
  patron saint of, 56–57
  ports of, 17
  regions of, 11–22
  size of, 10
  vegetation of, 19, 20
  wildlife of, 13, 14–15, 16
  see also specific regions
Argentina (Fodor's), 12
Argentina Handbook (Nurse), 19–20
Argentine Anticommunist Alliance (AAA), 42
Argentine Confederation, 29–30
arts
  dance, 69–70
  films, 72–73
  folk arts, 66
  literature, 68–69
  music, 71–72, 78
  painting, 67–68
  theater, 72
auto racing, 76
Avellaneda, Nicolas, 30

Bignone, Reynaldo, 46
Bigongiari, Diego, 12
Bolivia, 24, 26, 27–28
Buenos Aires, 18–19, 25, 26, 53
businesses
  farming, 62–63
  manufacturing, 19, 63, 64
  ranching, 62–63
  service, 63–64
  tourism, 12–13, 87

Cabot, Sebastian, 24
Castellano, 58
Castillo, Ramón S., 34
civil wars, 30
  see also political problems
colonial era, 24–25, 31
common market, Latin American, 47
constitution, 28–30
corruption, 31, 32, 48–49, 80–82, 86–87
coups, 32–34, 39, 43–45, 46
  see also political problems
cowboys. *See* gauchos
crops, 11–12, 15, 16, 17, 62–63
culture. *See* arts; customs; people
currency, 50, 64, 87–88
customs
  dancing, 69–70
  festivals, 76–79
  food, 61–62

holidays, 76–79
pilgrimages, 78
psychotherapy, 55
religion, 55–58
tango, 69–70, 78
yerba maté, 12, 14
  see also sports
Cuyo, 15–16

dance, 69–70
desaparecidos (disappeared
  ones), 44, 45
desert region, 13–14
Dirty War, 46–47
Duarte, Eva Maria. *See* Perón,
  Eva
Duhalde, Eduardo, 50

economic problems
  banking system, 85
  bank loan defaults, 49–50
  currency devaluation, 50, 64,
    87–88
  emigration, 83
  foreign debt, 85
  gap between rich and poor, 48
  immigrant workers, 64–65
  inflation, 37, 39, 46, 47, 50, 64
  international loans, 81–82
  poverty, 50, 54
  privatization of business, 88
  recession, 49, 82
  standard of living decline,
    80–81, 82
  unemployment, 46, 49, 64, 82,
    83–88
  world wars and, 32, 33
education system, 59–61
Evita. *See* Perón, Eva

factories, 19, 63, 64
Falkland Islands, 21, 22, 45–46
farming, 11–12
Farrell, Edelmiro, 34
films, 72–73

Fodor's, 12
folk arts, 66
folk music, 71–72, 78
food, 61–62
football. *See* soccer
Frondizi, Arturo, 39

Galtieri, Leopoldo, 46
Garay, Juan de, 25
gauchos, 59, 63, 68, 78
government. *See* history; political
  problems
Gran Chaco, 13–15
guerrillas, 40, 42
Guevara, Ernesto "Che," 40, 41

history
  civil wars, 30
  discovery, 24
  explorers, 24
  government problems, 31–33
  immigration and development,
    30–31
  independence, 27–28
  military coups, 32–34, 39,
    43–45, 46
  Nazis, 34
  settlement, 24–26
  Spanish colonial era, 24–27
  stability and growth, 30–31
  unification, 30
  world wars, 32–33
holidays, 76–79
human rights abuses, 43–45, 68

Igazú Falls, 12–13
Illia, Arturo, 39
immigration
  Asian, 52
  European, 51–52
  impact of, on character of na-
    tion, 30
  Latin American, 53
  Middle Eastern, 52
  of workers, 64–65

Inca, 23
independence, 27–30
indigenous people
  art of, 66
  dances of, 70
  destruction of, 30
  explorers and, 24
  mestizos, 52
  missionaries and, 24
  number of surviving, 52–53
  prehistoric, 23
  religious practices of, 55
  settlers and, 24–25, 26
  Spanish colonial era and, 24–25
industry, 19, 63, 64
Infamous Decade, 33
Irigoyen, Hipólito, 31–32

Jesuits, 24
jobs, 64–65
junta, 40
Justo, Augustín P., 33

language, 58–59
Las Malvinas. *See* Falkland Islands
Lavagna, Roberto, 50
leaders. *See* corruption; Peronism; political problems
literature, 68–69
livestock, 63

Magellan, Ferdinand, 24, 25
Malvinas Islands, 21–22
Maradona, Diego, 75
meal customs, 61–62
media, 72–73
Mendoza, Pedro de, 24, 26
Menem, Carlos Saúl, 47–49
Mercasur, 47
Mesopotamia (region of Argentina), 11–13
mestizos, 52, 58
middle class, 65
military coups, 32–34, 39, 43–45, 46

  see also political problems
mineral resources, 15
money. *See* economic problems
Montoneros, 40
Mothers of the Plaza del Mayo, 44, 45, 46
mountain areas, 15–16
movies, 72–73
music, 70–72

name, 10–11
national debt, 85
native tribes. *See* indigenous people
Nazis, 34
newspapers, 73
Nurse, Charlie, 19

Onganía, Juan Carlos, 40
opera, 70–71

painters, 66–67
Pampa, 16–17
Paraguay, 26, 27–28
Patagonia, 19–20
Peña, Roque Sáenz, 31
people
  clothing of, 59
  cultural diversity of, 51–55
  education system and, 59–61
  family life of, 61
  patriotism of, 55
  psychotherapy and, 55
  religious practices of, 55–57
  rural life of, 53–54
  urban life of, 53
Perón, Eva, 36–37, 38, 57–58
Perón, Isabel, 42–43
Perón, Juan
  death of, 42
  early political career of, 35–36
  exile of, 39
  military and, 37
  reforms of, 35, 37
  return of, to power, 40–42

suppression of freedoms under, 37

Peronism, 35–39

Peru, 24, 25

pilgrimages, 78

plains regions, 13–14, 16–17, 19–20

Plan of Economic Action (1933), 33

political problems

censorship, 73

corruption, 31, 32, 48–49, 80–82, 86–87

death squads, 43–45

desaparecidos (disappeared ones), 44, 45

internal power struggles, 85–86

leadership crisis, 50

military coups, 32–34, 39, 43–45, 46

repression, 43–45, 73

struggle between workers and military, 32, 39

war crimes, 46–47

polo, 75–76

Portugal, 24, 25

poverty, 50, 54

prehistory, 23

presidents. *See* corruption; Peronism; political problems

problems. *See* economic problems; political problems; social problems

products, 13–14, 15, 63

progress, 47–48, 80–81

Puna, 15

Radical Party, 31

Ramírez, Pedro, 34

ranching, 13, 16–17, 62–63

see also gauchos

rebels. *See* guerrillas

Rega, José López, 42

religion, 55–57, 77–78

repression, 37, 42–45

Rio de la Plata (United Provinces of), 28–30

Rio de la Plata (Viceroyalty of), 26–27

rivers, 11, 12–13, 18, 19

Roca, Julio A., 30

Roman Catholic Church, 55

Rosas, Juan Manuel de, 29

Rúa, Fernando de la, 49

Saa, Adolfo Rodriguez, 49

San Martín, José de, 28

San Nicolás Agreement, 29–30

Sarmiento, Domingo Faustino, 30

schools, 59–61

silver, 10, 25

slavery, 24, 26

soccer, 73–74, 75

Social Aid Foundation, 37

social problems

class differences, 53

class struggle, 31

crime, 84–85

drug trade, 65

emigration, 83

gap between rich and poor, 83

immigrant workers, 64–65

malnutrition, 83

middle class decline, 65

poverty, 50, 54

standard of living decline, 80–81, 82

unemployment, 46, 49, 64, 82, 83–88

Solís, Juan Díaz de, 24

Spanish colonial era, 24–25, 31

sports, 73–76

strikes, 49

tango, 69–70, 78

theater, 72

Tierra del Fuego, 10, 20–21

tourism, 12–13, 87

tropical regions, 11–13

Tulchin, Joseph S., 85

Uriburu, José F., 33
Uruguay, 26

vegetation, 11
Videla, Jorge Rafael, 43

wildlife, 13, 14–15, 16
work, 64–65
World War I, 32
World War II, 32–33

yerba maté, 12, 14

Picture Credits

ABOUT THE AUTHOR

Terri Dougherty is a freelance writer from Appleton, Wisconsin. In addition to nonfiction books for children, she also writes magazine and newspaper articles. A native of Black Creek, Wisconsin, Terri was a newspaper reporter and editor before beginning her freelance writing career. She enjoys traveling, soccer, and reading, as well as skiing and attending plays with her husband, Denis, and swimming, biking, and playing with their three children, Kyle, Rachel, and Emily.